A BEAUTIFU

A BEAUTIFUL VIEW

A Friendlier Christianity as a Way of Life

A GUIDE FOR GROUP OR INDIVIDUAL STUDY

F. Morgan Roberts

CASCADE *Books* • Eugene, Oregon

A BEAUTIFUL VIEW
A Friendlier Christanity as a Way of Life

Cascade Books
An Imprint of Wipf and Stock Publishers
199 W. 8th Ave., Suite 3
Eugene, OR 97401

www.wipfandstock.com

PAPERBACK ISBN: 978-1-5326-3577-9
HARDCOVER ISBN: 978-1-5326-3579-3
EBOOK ISBN: 978-1-5326-3578-6

Cataloguing-in-Publication data:

Names: Roberts, F. Morgan, author.
Title: A beautiful view : a friendlier Christanity as a way of life / F. Morgan
   Roberts.
Description: Eugene, OR: Cascade Books, 2018 | Includes bibliographical refer-
   ences.
Identifiers: ISBN 978-1-5326-3577-9 (paperback) | ISBN 978-1-5326-3579-3
   (hardcover) | ISBN 978-1-5326-3578-6 (ebook)
Subjects: LCSH: Theology, Doctrinal—Popular works.
Classification: BT 77 .R55 2018 (paperback) | BT 77 (ebook)

Manufactured in the U.S.A.   06/29/18

To John M. Mulder, beloved companion
along the Upward Way.

Contents

Acknowledgments

Without the encouragement of my friend, John Mulder, this book would not have been written. His confidence in me to undertake such a project, especially in this ninetieth year of my life, will never be forgotten.

The first draft of this book was shared with Pam Norvell, a member of Harvest United Methodist Church in Sarasota. Because of her previous editorial experience, and also her work with small study groups, her initial input was invaluable. The book has changed greatly in the months since then, but Pam was there in the beginning.

Pastor Stephen D. MacConnell and his Equipping Ministry Director, Carolyn Wilson, at Church of the Palms in Sarasota, made it possible for me to share five chapters of this book as a field test with some members of the congregation during the Lenten season. To those ninety-plus members whose enthusiasm and compelling questions gave me ideas that changed the shape of the original manuscript I am deeply indebted.

My dear wife Nora has proofed every page of this final version. Her microscopic attention to detail somehow detects errors that exceed the editing capabilities of my computer. A second reading was also done by my daughter, Holly Roberts Mouderres. I am blessed to have family members with such patience and skills.

I will donate all profits and royalties from this book to the Redlands Christian Migrant Association, 420 West Main Street, Immokalee, Florida. Through its two charter schools in Immokalee and Wimauma and its eighty-seven child care centers, it serves more than 8,000 farmworker children annually. It has been my privilege to work with some of these students and their devoted teachers over the past eleven years.

Introduction

This little book started out as an idea of my friend and former coauthor, John Mulder. His suggestion was that I consider writing a study guide about Christian beliefs that he could use with a group of men with whom he meets weekly at his church. He wanted a book of about twelve chapters that could be studied and discussed over a three-month period. As mentioned in my acknowledgements, I was offered an opportunity to share five of its chapters with a live audience during Lent at the church I attend. I accepted this offer enthusiastically because I wanted to give my ideas a "field test" with members of a church like the one that John attends.

Attendance held up well during those five weeks; the discussions and questions were lively and friendly, with varying viewpoints aired. Almost every week someone would ask, "When will this book be published?" This was, of course, encouraging, but I realized that this would demand more work on my original manuscript, because my book was turning out to be more about a way of life than a study of beliefs. What we believe, of course, shapes how we live; however, it began to appear that the title might be more inviting if it indicated that we're talking more about life than about theology. And that is how I have arrived at the present title.

This book can be used not only with groups, but also for personal study and devotion. Some ideas for reflection, discussion, and additional reading will be offered at the end of the book. However you may be using it, my hope is that it will help you enter into the experience of what I have called "a friendlier Christianity." If what I'm saying has an air of superiority, suggesting that my idea of Christianity is friendlier than yours, and that your faith needs fixing, then let me assure you that it is not my intention to "fix" anyone. I need too much fixing myself to assume such a stance. However, after over a half-century of ministry, and now as the shadows lengthen on life's long day, I do believe that our world could experience some healing from a friendlier faith. For that matter, I believe that Christ's presence is pursuing every life and leading each one of us, in different ways, in that direction. We'll be talking more about how this is happening as we move on. So, if any of this sounds interesting, read on.

Chapter 1

The Goal

A Friendlier Faith

I hope that my book will help us to rewire our hearts and minds with a friendlier, Christlike faith. It's hard to argue with such a goal. Even members of other faiths (or no faith) who have no intention of embracing Christianity wish that Christians, in both belief and behavior, were more authentically like the Jesus who is often portrayed, even in some popular songs, as the friend of little children. Jesus is *not* the problem; the problem is with the people who profess to be his followers. One of my former associate pastors who died of AIDS had a favorite bumper sticker that expressed what he had to endure from many "true-believer" Christians during his long illness. It said, "God, please save me from your followers."

It is because of such unfriendly versions of our faith that I am struggling to express what it might be like if we could develop a kindlier Christianity. For that matter, I think my book is about a more contemplative and beautiful view of life, one lived on a higher plateau where, moment by moment, we live breathing what someone once called, "the keen bracing air of those silent mountains where God is known."

To begin at the beginning, let's look at the friendly faith of Jesus as it was displayed in the first sermon he delivered in his hometown synagogue in Nazareth (Luke 4:16–19). His Scripture lesson was from Isaiah, but listen to what he read: "The Spirit of the Lord is upon me, because he has anointed me to bring good news to the poor. He has sent me to proclaim release to the captives and recovery of sight to the blind, to let the oppressed go free, to proclaim the year of the Lord's favor." That's where the Scripture reading ended, where he rolled up the scroll and began to preach. But wait, there's something missing because, when we check our Bibles, we find that he had omitted Isaiah's last words which read, "and the day of vengeance of our God" (Isa 61:2). Jesus hadn't come to talk about a vengeful God, and felt free to edit and reinterpret Holy Scripture! If we continue to follow Jesus' teaching, it becomes apparent that he felt free to read Scripture critically in terms of his own vision of God as a friendly father. Jesus consistently ignored large portions of Hebrew Scripture in which God is depicted as an angry, violent, and unfriendly tyrant. So much for the notion that all Scripture is equally "authoritative Scripture"! It certainly wasn't that for Jesus.

Moving on from Jesus into what we learn about the faith of the earliest Christians, we see the same radical faith in a God who upended the unfriendly power of the Roman Empire. Notice what we see. Because Jesus had been raised from the dead, everything had changed. The resurrection was the undeniable sign that God was now in charge. Caesar was no longer king of kings, and the followers of Jesus were now citizens of another kingdom, the kingdom of God, and their allegiance was to King Jesus. The agenda of the early church was to bring the friendly rule of God to earth. Their basic prayer expressed that agenda: "Thy kingdom come, thy will be done on earth." Early Christianity was involved, not in escaping hell and getting into heaven, but in bringing God's heavenly rule down to earth, especially for the multitudes for whom life on earth was hellish. If you don't get this main point, you've missed the whole point!

All of the ancient, cruel distinctions were gone. As Paul wrote, "There is no longer Jew or Greek, there is no longer slave and free, there is no longer male and female; for all of you are one in Christ Jesus" (Gal 3:28). Or in another letter, "There is no longer Greek and Jew, circumcised and uncircumcised, barbarian, Scythian, slave and free, but Christ is all and in all!" (Col 3:11). This was the end of harsh dualistic and divisive thinking about our life, the end of saved/lost, good guy/bad guy thinking.

Early Christianity was a cheerful, joyful, friendly faith, a stark contrast to the world of Roman oppression in which it was born, a world characterized by slavery, poverty, cruelty, and debauchery. In the midst of such darkness, early Christians believed not only that God had come to earth in Jesus to live with us humans, but also that God in Christ *was* living in all of us. When John wrote that "the Word became flesh" (John 1:14), he meant all flesh. Their Christ was a cosmic, universal Christ. When God took on human flesh in the life of Jesus, God was showing us what had always been true from the beginning: that we are all (and have always been) the children of God. We bear the image of God. Our physical bodies are God's sanctuary, temples of the Holy Spirit.

It was an entirely different and inclusive worldview. Paul said, "From now on, therefore, we regard no one from a human point of view" because "God was in Christ, reconciling the world to himself" (2 Cor 5:26–19). Just listen to the preaching of Peter and Paul in Acts. Peter goes to the home of a Roman centurion and begins his sermon by saying, "I truly understand that God shows no partiality, but in every nation anyone who fears him and does what is right is acceptable to him. You know the message he sent to the people of Israel, preaching peace by Jesus Christ—he is Lord of all" (Acts 10:34–36). And then Paul preaches to the Athenians and says, "Indeed, he [God] is not far from any of us. For in him we live and move and have our being; as even some of your own poets have said, 'For we too are his offspring'" (Acts 17:27–28). Their message was that we are all in Christ; God's incarnation in Christ has made it clear that we are all what we have always been since the dawn of creation, children of God. The apostolic message called all people to be what they *already* were: precious children of God!

No wonder Rome went after them; their message was treasonous. God, instead of Caesar, was running the show. Every life had dignity in Christ. Slavery as an economic system was being undermined. The Roman way of life was being challenged. The very fact that early Christians were persecuted proves that their agenda was threatening. If the usual heaven/hell agenda had been their message, Rome would never have bothered them. If the message of the early church had been "pie in the sky by and by," Rome would have been delighted; such a new religion would keep the enslaved multitudes pacified by the future hope of heaven. Obviously, that wasn't the message of the early church. Instead, the proclamation of the universal kingdom of God and the end of all distinctions was a dangerous gospel and needed to be crushed.

But nothing could crush the friendly, joyful spirit of the early Christians. They believed that we are living in a world made lovely by Christ's pervading presence. And that is the way of life that I hope to inspire and revive. I hope that you, finally, will arrive at a "beautiful view" of this Christ-haunted, enchanted world in which we're living. That's where we'll be going in the coming chapters.

Chapter 2

Where It All Began

I need to begin by telling you "where I'm coming from" because if it hadn't begun *where* and *how* it did, I wouldn't be writing this book—or any book—and my life would have been something entirely different from what it turned out to be. I was raised in a neighborhood with a beautiful view; that's why it was called Bellevue. However, except for the good and simple people who were my neighbors, the view was the only beautiful thing about Bellevue. We lived at the far end of the city, as close to the countryside as you could get without being out of the city. I don't know who gave Bellevue its name, but suspect that it was because it was located on a plateau from which, if I walked across the street and up the hill, I could enjoy a magnificent view of a historic valley. I've never been able to get that vista out of my heart. Harry Truman had to work at remembering where he came from. He once said, "I tried never to forget who I was and where I'd come from." It hasn't been that way for me; I've never forgotten where I came from. Bellevue has always been in my heart, even though most people would never brag about being from Bellevue.

Despite its fancy name, Bellevue was definitely blue collar. Down the street there was a nice little public park, but up the street it was different. In three short blocks, one came to a German beer-drinking park for the many soccer-loving Germans in our neighborhood. Next to their park was "the big blue house." It was a brothel; why it was allowed to operate, and how it got there I don't know. Maybe it was because our neighborhood was on the far west end of the city where, in past years, there had been a harness racing track, which would have drawn the gambling, drinking crowd. Despite the presence of that "house of ill repute," our neighborhood was a decent place to live. People took good care of their little homes, and children were safe to play on the streets. So, the bordello was an embarrassment for us. Its customers came from other parts of town, or from out of town. Thus, the residents of Bellevue ignored it, and went about their plain way of life, most of them working daily at what was called "the plant."

Bellevue was located at the edge of a thriving industrial city where, during World War II, materials for the war effort were being manufactured. However, it was the work going on in those factories that got me, as a city boy, out into the country. Because the real country boys on small farms had come to the city to earn bigger money at the factories, those small farms had to accept such help as they could get from boys who lived on the edge of the cities. I was one such teenager who peddled out and back every day on my bicycle to earn an hourly wage of thirty-five cents, pitching hay and doing other farm chores, all of which I enjoyed, especially on this particular farm that was still being worked in the old-fashioned way with horses instead of tractors. Because I had no vocational or college plans, I thought that life in the country on a farm would be something I'd enjoy, even though such a life would hardly ever be possible for me. How could I ever accumulate enough money to buy a farm? It would make more sense for me to stay in the city and work in the same factory where my father, cousins, and uncles would spend most of their lives.

The plant had given them a good life, despite their lack of education. None of my parents, uncles, or aunts had ever been encouraged to finish school. My maternal grandmother was illiterate and couldn't even sign her name on her wedding license in 1869. My paternal grandparents also were mostly illiterate; my paternal grandfather, in the days before the "horseless carriage," was a street sweeper. But even with these limitations, both the men and women of this immigrant family from South Wales had been able to find stable employment, in the earliest years in the iron mill in a nearby city, or in the collar shop (where my mother was a button-hole stitcher). Later on, they all moved to our city, and worked at the plant, where they were enjoying the American dream of home ownership. So, there was a sensible, available future for me. I could enjoy a semi-rural life without working on a farm. In the valley below our neighborhood there were woods in which to roam, plus a stream for fishing and trapping. Having no other goals, that would be my life—or so I was thinking in 1944. But it all began to change one night when I heard Roy Acuff singing a ballad entitled "A Prodigal Son."

On every Saturday night, at exactly 10:30 PM, I would sit in my attic bedroom and tune in radio station WSM Nashville, via WWVA Wheeling, to hear my favorite program, the Grand Ole Opry. This was the original Opry, before today's glitzier version from Opryland. It came from the old Ryman Auditorium in Nashville, and featured Roy Acuff and the Smoky Mountain Boys. Back then, such music was not called "country," but "hillbilly." My high school friends would have been enjoying 1940s big band music, perhaps at a dance or at some soda fountain on a jukebox. But for some reason, I stayed home on Saturday nights for this broadcast. And on one special night, I heard Roy Acuff singing "A Prodigal Son." Later I played the 78-rpm recording of that song so many times that I can still sing most of the lyrics from memory. However, remembering those words this many years later, I cannot imagine why I was so captivated by them.

I was not like that prodigal son who had strayed from his family home to a faraway country where, in the words of the King James Version, he had "wasted his substance with riotous living" (Luke 15:18). And I was certainly not, as the song promised, looking for Jesus to descend from the sky to wash all my sins away. My sins were the usual small stuff of a teenager, but not so troublesome as to want them washed away. I was not burdened by any fear of dying, nor had I any interest in going home to heaven as in the longing words of the song, even though several of the older boys from my high school had gone off to war, never to return. I still can't explain what drew me to that ballad, unless it was a certain *sehnsucht*, a longing for some kind of homecoming. Most interesting of all, I didn't know that the song had some connection with a parable of Jesus.

However, some time after hearing that ballad, there was a crucial coincidence. I wasn't even looking for it, but in those same months in which I was accumulating a large pile of 78-rpm Roy Acuff recordings, I "happened" to find an old leather-bound New Testament in my attic bedroom—or better yet, maybe it found me! This doesn't sound like an extraordinary find. There must have been a Bible downstairs among my parents' possessions. They belonged to a church but, like many blue-collar families during the Great Depression, had ceased from being regular churchgoers. Thus, my exposure to church or Sunday school was very limited. During my high school years I was a happy, though unchurched, teenager. But now this discovery became all-important.

This New Testament had belonged to my Aunt Susan, whose signature was on the flyleaf with the date of 1900. What I cannot recall or explain is how I managed to locate Luke's so-called parable of the Prodigal Son (Luke 15: 11–32). As I type these words, that same frayed and worn New Testament sits on my desk, and it contains no useful notes or indices that would have helped me find the parable—but somehow, I did. What is even more beyond explanation is why I memorized the entire parable—verbatim! There was no reward for Scripture memorization to encourage such a feat. But for that matter, I didn't stop there; I began memorizing other passages, a record of which I kept on the back flyleaf, even though I cannot explain why I chose those passages. Of course, I didn't tell anyone what I was doing. There was no reason to tell my parents; I was a normal teenager, enjoying my privacy. And I certainly didn't tell my friends at high school, lest I be considered some kind of religious freak.

But finally, I did tell someone. There was assigned seating in our twelfth-grade biology class, and seated behind me was an infectiously friendly girl named Doris. She was everything that we call winsome (which most girls don't want to be called). We never dated. It was just fun talking with her, especially because she wanted to become a missionary. She never did become one, unless you might regard her main missionary work as that of being focused on me. She never "witnessed" to me about being saved. We just talked as I asked questions until, on one day, I told her that I was memorizing Scripture. And as they say, "the rest is history."

Shortly thereafter, I began attending her church. It was a se-verely legalistic, fundamentalist congregation. Movies, dancing, card-playing, drinking, smoking, and lipstick were strictly taboo. The pastor was a humorless authoritarian, who seemed to labor under some heavy burden of shame or blame. His ministry could have been likened to a travel agency that specialized in guilt trips. But the people of the church, as is often the case, were somehow better and kinder than the faith they professed to believe. And they believed in this churchless kid whom Doris had brought to church. They prayed for me and, as the dying Arthur said, "More things are wrought by prayer than this world dreams of."

And that gloomy pastor? He did one thing that made all the difference in my future: for some reason, he assigned me to the tutelage of a retired missionary who began tutoring me—at age seventeen—in New Testament Greek! It set the direction for my college studies and my eventual graduation with high honors in classical Greek. And I can't even take credit for that academic ac-complishment because, despite the advice of the church members that I should attend a so-called Christian college or Bible school, my cousin Edwin exerted his influence to ensure that I attended the university where he was a professor. And he, as an orphaned teenager, had similarly been saved by the amazing grace and gen-erosity of an anonymous benefactor who, recognizing his poten-tial, had paid for his college education. It was all "grace upon grace upon grace" that landed cousin Edwin (and later me) at Colgate University. More importantly, the tutoring I received from the old missionary became the beginning of a lifelong journey into the deeper meaning of this parable—not the parable of a prodigal son, but more accurately the parable of a wastefully merciful, prodigal Father. It's the final scene in the parable that matters most. For that matter, what makes all the difference in our lives is how we think about the final scene, how the story ends—and that's where we'll begin in the next chapter as we look more closely at the parable.

Chapter 3

We Know How
the Story Ends

Several years ago, a *New York Times* reporter interviewed Dr. Calvin Butts, pastor of the famous Abyssinian Baptist Church in Harlem. Set within a neighborhood scarred by drugs, poverty, gang warfare, and other related problems, his congregation provides a wide variety of healing ministries. After the pastor described those works of community outreach, the reporter inquired, "Do you think your church is making a real difference?" When Dr. Butts replied that he really couldn't prove their effectiveness, the reporter asked, "So why do you keep on doing them?" I have always been moved by Dr. Butts' response; he said, "Because we read the Bible, and we know how the story ends."

How do *you* think the human story ends? Where is our life headed? Our answer to that question is all-important because, although we may not be aware of it, our answer determines the way in which we live our life in the present. Some of you know that the study of the story's ending is the department of theology called eschatology, derived from the Greek adjective, *eschatos*, meaning "last" or "final." We may not realize it, but we are all living in terms of a "personal" eschatology. Consciously or unconsciously, we live in a certain way and make certain choices because we have been wired with some notion of where life is headed. Indeed, we have been wired so effectively that what we *say* we believe can be constantly denied by the *way* in which we are living. The way we *walk*, not the way we *talk*, reveals what we really believe about the end of the story. Let's look at a hypothetical example.

Some popular preacher/author focuses upon the Rapture and how we need to be ready for this final moment of separation and judgement. The core of his message is "turn or burn, get right or get left." However, when we look more closely at his life, we discover that he does not *walk* his *talk*. The royalties from his books and income from his TV ministry allow him to live in the countryside on an opulent ranch, with a collection of fine horses and expensive sports cars. Obviously, his real eschatology is not in his *talk* about the Rapture. Instead, he believes that life is a contest at the end of which whoever has the most toys wins. That's what he really believes about the end of the story. What we say we believe can be denied by the way we live.

So where do you think it's all headed? And what did Jesus see as the end of the story? The parable of the Prodigal Son ends with a gala, welcome-home banquet, with sounds of music and dancing and the appetizing aromas of feasting. God is depicted in this parable as a father who is unconditionally welcoming. When the older brother stands outside, refusing to party with his younger brother who has been forgiven by an extravagant, wasteful mercy, the father leaves the party and stands outside, pleading with him to join the party. This parable might better have been called the parable of the Prodigal God. Surely, Jesus has given us the picture of a God who is "endlessly, foolishly, and incredibly merciful." We see the same image of a welcoming God in a previous passage in Luke.

One day, when Jesus' disciples asked, "Lord, will only a few be saved?" he told them that we're headed toward a much bigger banquet than our minds can conceive. He said, "People will come from east and west, and from north and south, and sit at table in the kingdom of God" (Luke 13:29). Someday, the Heavenly Shepherd will bring all the sheep home, even the ones whom Jesus called the "other" sheep. In many churches, the only time when we hear those words about the great heavenly banquet is when we celebrate Holy Communion. As we begin the celebration of that sacrament, the officiant will repeat Jesus' words about such a worldwide banquet.

At other times, however, what we may hear from the *pulpit* is different from what we have heard at the communion *table*. Instead of hearing about God's open invitation to the great banquet, we hear sermons in which God is not the welcoming father who stands *outside* the homecoming banquet hall, urging even his *reluctant son* to join the party. We hear instead about a *reluctant God* who stands *inside* the door of the banquet hall, demanding certain credentials of belief and behavior before allowing admission to the party. Because of such imagery of a reluctant God, a large number of church people (Protestant, Catholic, or Orthodox) have come to believe that the church's role is that of a gatekeeper who determines who will escape hell and enter heaven. After listening to people over many years of ministry, my guess is that even many people outside of the church believe that such a gatekeeping ministry is the church's main agenda (which may be why many of them have left the church!).

The best way to begin rewiring our minds with a friendlier faith is by noticing that the heaven/hell agenda was not the main agenda of either Jesus or Paul. Isn't it rather odd that, in the prayer Jesus taught us to pray, there is no mention of going to heaven or escaping hell? Instead, Jesus taught us to pray for the coming of God's rule (kingdom) on earth. If we follow Jesus' agenda, we'll stop worrying about getting into heaven *after* we die, and start working now *before* we die to make earth heavenly for the world's poor. Paul has the same concern. If we could have lunch with Paul and ask him to tell us about hell, he wouldn't know what we were talking about because, instead of reading Paul's letters carefully, we have read into them the images of Dante's *Inferno*, which wasn't written until many centuries later (AD 1320).

So, the main message of the parable is at the very end, and it focuses upon the older brother and his reluctance to join the banquet. In my teenage reading of the parable, I had missed this major point. Could it be that God's amazing grace is so universal that certain people, like the older brother, will refuse to enter the great banquet of the kingdom? It's the older brother who needs our attention. I'd like to hear the conversation going on out there in the darkness. When his father comes out, pleading with him to come in, I hear him saying, "Me, come to a party like that? That son of *yours* (not my brother) comes dragging home, smelling like a Gentile hog farm and a big-city brothel, and you're carrying on like it's the second coming!" Do you see what this scene is saying? We've always been given the scenario of a final judgement in which, because of bad beliefs and behavior, the door is slammed shut, and the bad guys are left outside. Traditionally, in sermons (and even in jokes), upon our arrival at the pearly gates, Saint Peter administers a two-part exam. First is a multiple-choice exam on theology to test our beliefs. Next is a background check about our behavior. If we pass, we're admitted; if we fail, the gates close, and we're flushed down the drain into the sewer of hell.

But this parable stands our traditional picture upside down and tells us, instead, that no one is locked out, that the door is always open to the heavenly banquet—but that some people won't want to come in because they don't like the motley crew that God has accepted in grace and mercy. Evidently, when some people discover how "foolishly merciful" God can be, that "there's a wideness in God's mercy, like the wideness of the sea"—they won't want to come in. But the mind-blowing picture with which we are left is that, even if such proud prigs stand outside the great banquet, our wastefully merciful Father is standing outside with them. Or to put it in the words of one of Fred Rogers's songs for little children, "You can never go down the drain."

Is the older brother's problem the demand for his own private heavenly club? Is the essence of hell the desire to be left alone? G. A. Studdert Kennedy's poem gets at very heart of this hellish, private notion of heaven.

IF I HAD A MILLION POUNDS
I would buy me a perfect island home,
Sweet set in a southern sea,
And there would I build me a paradise
For the heart o' my Love and me.
I would plant me a perfect garden there,
The one that my dream soul knows,
And the years would flow as the petals grow,
That flame to a perfect rose.
I would build me a perfect temple there,
A shrine where my Christ might dwell,
And then would I wake to behold my soul
Damned deep in a perfect Hell.

Our prodigal God will let no one be an outsider; the wide circle of God's grace encompasses everyone. God is always present with those who appear to stand outside, with those who seem to reject divine love and mercy. But because our prodigal God has set such endless, merciful boundaries, heaven and hell have become the same place! No wonder we sing at Eastertide (probably without noticing what we've been singing), "He closed the yawning gates of Hell; The bars from Heaven's high portals fell: Let hymns of praise His triumphs tell. Alleluia!" On the day of resurrection, there was an unbelievably universal redistricting of boundary lines. Heaven was enlarged to encompass hell, as our triumphant Christ, having descended into hell, led the captive souls in hell into the bounds of heaven. So, hell is closed! You can't go there any longer! You can stand at the edge of heaven, just as the elder brother stood outside the banquet hall; however, our wastefully merciful Father stands out there with you, calling endlessly, and reminding you, "Child, you are always with me, and all that is mine is yours" (Luke 15:31).

Someone asks, "But is there no punishment for the wicked?" Good question! And the answer is a resounding "yes." After all, there are people who become monsters of iniquity. The recently discovered diaries of Heinrich Himmler, the SS chief who meticulously planned the mass killing of millions of Jews, reveals that, on one day, he witnessed the gassing of 400 women and girls—and then attended a banquet of SS officers! Can such sick wickedness ever be forgiven?

Let me state it this way: the wicked are punished eternally, but in the hell of God's endlessly loving presence. I still recall Ernie Campbell saying, "They all come home at last; there's no place else to go." What is heaven for the righteous is hell for the wicked—and it is eternally inescapable until they decide to start breathing it's loving atmosphere. It is hell until they make it their heaven. To suggest, as do some hell-fire preachers, that there is a "place of endless, conscious, eternal torment" outside the presence of God is to deny the infinity and omnipresence of God. As the Shorter Catechism states, "God is a Spirit, infinite, eternal, and unchangeable, in his being, wisdom, power, holiness, justice, goodness, and truth." You can't ever get outside of an infinite and omnipresent God.

And so, we all, finally, go into the presence of God, because there's no place else to go. We are now, and always will be, in the presence of God. But in the world to come we will not carry with us the trappings of the small, false, ego-bound self in which we all, to some extent have lived our present life. Our fancy clothes, cars, and homes will be left behind. The symbols of our status, our money, our positions, our titles, and our degrees will no longer set us apart from the rest of the human family. All that will matter is whether we've become the calm, kind, quiet, friendly, gentle, humble, helpful, and hopeful persons we're meant to be. That's the only clothing of heaven. Without such clothing, we will be naked and exposed—but still surrounded by inescapable love. For such naked souls, it will be a cold hell until it becomes a warmly loving heaven. And the "hell of it" for the naked is that there can be no escape. They have spent their lives running away from much of the human family, or worse yet, using or abusing the great unwashed multitudes. But now there is no escape.

The godless woman of wealth will now be poor and naked in the presence of her poverty-stricken cleaning woman, who is now clothed in spiritual splendor, still singing those songs of praise that sustained her during her earthly pilgrimage. Indeed, it will be hell for that godless rich lady—and there's no escape because God's heavenly presence is all there is. What is heaven for her cleaning woman has become, for her, a constant hell. However, she is not left alone in her misery, because her former cleaning woman stands by her, urging her to join in on the singing, just as the prodigal Father stood by his proud son in the outer darkness, urging him to join the banquet.

Will such naked, godless residents, who must remain forever in the pure hell of heaven, ever accept the invitation to join the great banquet? To that question there is no infallible answer. One of my dear scholarly friends believes that, when we die and pass into the inescapable presence of God, we will be changed immediately by the fiery love of God. We will see that this beatific vision was what we were always seeking and embrace it immediately, repenting of our evil past, begging forgiveness of those we've harmed, and receiving their forgiveness. For now, however, the parable comes to an end, but without telling us whether the older son ever decided to join the party.

But I imagine another possible ending, and it includes a character left out of the original story: the mother of the two sons. Just as we leave the old farmer, standing outside the banquet hall with his reluctant son, I picture something else happening. My guess is that shortly thereafter, the old mother said to the younger son, "OK. You're enjoying your party, but take a break now, and get out there and help your dad talk to your brother." So now the younger brother goes out to join his father. Then, shortly after that, the old mother comes out herself and joins them. So, there they stand in the darkness, the father, the son, and the mother—the Father, the Son, and the Mothering Spirit, a perfect Trinity of amazing grace. Because of the grace of our Lord Jesus Christ, and the love of God, and the ministry of the Holy Spirit, could anyone ever be left behind?

It would seem logical at this point to move into a discussion of the holy family of the Trinity, but that can wait for a future chapter because I'm running ahead of some of my readers. Having walked in their shoes during my early years in a strict, fundamentalist church, I know that there are two matters that must be addressed for them before we can move on. Two questions need to be explored: (1) What happened in the garden of Eden? (2) What happened on the cross? So here we go on to those questions.

Chapter 4

The Good News from the Garden of Eden

Whenever I read the story of what happened in the garden of Eden, I think of Garrison Keillor as he ends his weekly news report from the legendary town of Lake Wobegon, "And that's the news from Lake Wobegon." The news that comes to us in the Bible's story about the garden of Eden is, in some ways, like the blend we encounter in Lake Wobegon. It's a sympathetic mixture of the good and the bad, the wonder and worry of what it means to be human.

That is *not*, however, in my experience, the way it is presented in many sermons that I've heard over the years. I'm sure you've heard such sermons in which we're told that what started out good in the first chapter of the book of Genesis somehow took a bad turn in the third chapter. I can remember sermons in which it was said that what happened in Genesis 3 casts a long, dark shadow over the rest of the entire Bible. It is interpreted as the story of *The fall* and *original sin*, after which all of us, from the moment of our birth, as descendants of Adam and Eve, are infected by their disobedience as lost and fallen sinners. Let's try putting such ideas on the back burner as we look more closely at what *did* and *didn't* happen in the garden of Eden. Hopefully, by the end of this lesson, we'll see that the news from Eden's garden just might be very helpful!

Let's begin by recognizing that the creation stories in Genesis are not historical accounts. Many of us have been taught to think about them as such, but just a bit of reflection should remind us that the reliability of historical accounts requires verification by eyewitnesses, or else written evidence based upon the testimony of eyewitnesses. Obviously, no one was present to witness the creation of the first man and woman. There were no other people on earth to record the story. Neither newspaper reporters nor TV cameras were present to record the opening moments of the human story. Of course, you can resort to all kinds of theories to support the historicity of the stories, such as saying that, centuries later, God revealed to Moses the details of what happened. But the Bible never tells us that such a revelation ever took place; it's just someone's theory to justify their interpretation of these events as historical.

It is far more helpful to think of the creation stories as myths that were passed down over many centuries and, finally, reduced to writing many centuries later. The linguistic features of the Genesis stories indicate that they come from a time many centuries removed from the happenings in the stories. However, that does not mean that they are not true in a deeper sense. Unfortunately, we have come to associate the word *myth* with untruth. But the real purpose of myth is to tell us about *truth that is deeper than historical fact*. The deeper truth conveyed by myth might better be called *wisdom*. We've all shared myths with our children that teach them wisdom. I've lost count of the number of times I've told the story of Goldilocks and the Three Bears to granddaughter Madison. She knows it's not factual, but she'll never forget it and, hopefully, will remember the lesson it teaches: "Never mess around in an empty house whose owners you don't know!" So, let's return to the creation myths in Genesis with this deeper understanding of myth in mind.

You don't need to be a Hebrew scholar to recognize that there are two separate creation narratives in Genesis. Eden is not mentioned in the first story (Gen 1:1—2:4), but the newly created earth is a wonderful garden offering all kinds of plants, trees, birds, fish, cattle, and other animals. In the first account, everything is orderly and good, "indeed, very good." With such a sense of satisfaction, God takes the next day off (Gen 2:2), so that the account ends with no problems in God's new world. Biblical scholars mostly agree that it was written after the second account in chapter 3, probably during the Babylonian captivity, and that its main purpose was to highlight the identity of the Jewish people and remind them of the importance of retaining their identity by keeping the Sabbath. What is clear is that humans are created in the image of God, and that they are to enjoy their own Sabbath rest with God. Before we move on, however, we need to take notice of three important matters.

The first is a great affirmation that we must make regardless of what we believe may or may not have happened in chapter 3. A first-century rabbi name Paul stated in this way, "Long before he laid down earth's foundations, he had us in mind, had settled on us as the focus of his love, to be made whole and holy by his love. Long, long ago he decided to adopt us into his family through Jesus Christ. (What a pleasure he took in planning this!)" (Eph 1:4–5, *The Message*). Whatever happened in Eden could never thwart God's eternal determination to bring all of us into God's adopted family of grace. Nothing can take from us our original identity as having been created in the image of God. We are still, and always have been, God's children, bearing God's image and likeness.

The next amazing fact about the second creation story is that it appears to have been forgotten in the rest of Hebrew Scripture. Except for an uncertain and obscure reference in Ezekiel 28, the story does not cast a long shadow over the rest of the Bible's story, as many preachers often say that it does. It is not repeated as a recurrent reminder of what went wrong in Eden.

The third amazing fact is that there are two big words missing from the story. The words *sin* and *fall* are never mentioned in the story. Thus, there is no literal, scriptural basis in this story for making it the foundation for such doctrines as *original sin* or *the fall.*

Such doctrines must be read into the story. So, what happened? Let's come at this story from another angle.

In November 1993, I delivered a sermon entitled "The Perfect Teenager." It was on a Sunday designated as Youth Sunday, when many parents of our young people would be present. Teenagers read the Scripture lessons and offered prayers, while others acted as ushers; however, I was the preacher. What I said that morning was that, thanks to modern robotic technology, we can now enjoy having a perfect teenager. You can guess what I described as the advantages. We can build one starting at any chosen age, whether at the middle school or high school level, and our perfect teenager can be periodically updated. Just think of the wonderful possibilities. We can program your perfect child with whatever skills we desire. We can have a musical child without having to endure the arguments over practicing regularly, or having to listen to the agonizing sounds of their early efforts on the violin. We can also create a business model, a child who will be able to follow in the father's footsteps and, at the right time, take over leadership of the family business. If you want a scientific genius, just pick the department of science in which you want them to excel. And, of course, we can add to all of the above the perfect athlete; just pick your favorite sport.

Added to these, there are all the daily, practical benefits. No more arguing or talking back. No more need to keep after them, no more tensions about when they'll arrive home on weekend nights, and no more worry about the bad characters they choose as friends. And at the end of the teen years, they will attend the college of *your* choice, not *theirs*. You can think of many more blessings that will be yours if you opt for such a perfect teenager.

But, of course, there's a huge problem with such a perfect teenager. There's something missing in this robotic child, and the quality that's missing is that such a child can never give you what we're all seeking; such a perfect teenager can never give you love. Love can exist only between two persons who are perfectly free to choose to love (or not love) one another. Freedom of choice is what makes love possible. You can program perfect performance and unwavering mechanical response to instructions in a robotic child, but you cannot program love. Love can exist only between two free and unpredictable persons who, in utter freedom, have chosen to love one another. But, of course, the freedom to choose to love is, by definition, the freedom to choose *not* to love. Our freedom of choice makes life a risky venture. If you want to avoid having your heart broken, don't ever take such a risk; don't let any real child (or person) into your life.

But God took that huge risk! Instead of devising perfectly automated bipeds who would behave in a predictable manner, God took the gigantic risk of creating free and unpredictable children who could choose to enter into a fully voluntary and personal participation in God's great dance of love. God installed a dangerous "chip" in these teenagers; it was called freedom of choice.

So, if we return to the story of what happened in Eden with all of this in mind, the man and woman look more like teenagers who have graduated from the innocence of early childhood into the world of adult decision-making. When we hear the words, "You *may* eat freely of every tree of the garden; but of the tree of the knowledge of good and evil *you shall not* eat" (Gen 2:16–17), the very fact that man and woman are warned tells us that obedience was not programmed automatically into humankind; loving obedience must be chosen. Isn't that very fact a kind of good news that comes to us from the garden of Eden? We are hard-wired with the freedom to make good choices; we can choose to have a positive relationship with God.

But as the story proceeds, obedience is not chosen; they eat of the forbidden fruit that will give them the knowledge that belongs only to God, the knowledge of good and evil—and there is our perennial problem! We tend to want to be like God, knowing the distinction between good and evil. With such knowledge, we can take control of our safety and security. We can know the good guys from the bad guys, the saved from the lost, know who's "us" from "them." We can decide who's in and who's out, creating our own little safe circles, building walls that will protect "us" from "them." What we did not foresee was that, within our little circles and behind our high walls, we would always live in fear. It is no accident that, having eaten of the forbidden fruit, our first words to the gracious God who comes seeking us are, "I heard the sound of you in the garden, and I was *afraid*" (Gen 3:10).

This is the first mention of fear in the Bible—and it may tell us why, as we move on in the Bible's story, the most frequent command in all Scripture is "Fear not!" By the bad choice we made in Eden, and by the same bad choices we *continue* to make in eating of the forbidden fruit of *making distinctions*, we continue to be children of fear. We can understand why, given this dark possibility in our human nature, so much religion thereafter has been fear-based.

But there's an aspect of the Eden story that we must consider. When God took the risk of giving us freedom of choice, didn't God know ahead of time that we might make bad choices? For that matter, do we ever become mature adults without the experience of having made mistakes, bad choices? Even if this story happened zillions of years ago, it sounds like a story we could have written ourselves. How else could we grow up into the complicated world of adulthood if we didn't experience the pain of bad choices? To become persons who can choose to love what is good, we must taste the alternatives; only by making mistakes and becoming imperfect can we become free lovers of God and one another.

This is truly our story, a story that tells us how things always have been and still are—and best of all, a story about God's unceasing love for all of us, not as fallen sinners, but instead as imperfect teenagers. Surprisingly, it appears we may have stumbled in an upward direction, and that what happened was not so much the *original sin*, but the *original blessing*, with the woman acting as the heroine of this story in which we tumbled upward from the innocence of childhood and landed in a more blessed state of grace. That may be why such theologians as Augustine, Aquinas, and Ambrose called this a story of *the blessed sin (felix culpa)* that brought more good to humanity than would have been the case if we had remained in a state of innocence. There's a song in heaven that the angels cannot sing, a song that we alone as imperfect and forgiven children can sing, and that's the song "Amazing Grace."

So, as the story continues, it continues to be one that we could have written ourselves because it is so much like our story. With what they had learned about the consequences of bad decisions, it was time for the teenagers to move out of Eden's garden. It is as though God was saying, "No more free room and board! Get a job, earn a living by the sweat of your brow, pay your own car insurance! Settle down, get married, and have children, because there's nothing like having your own children that will really help you to grow up."

So, they moved out to live where we all live, east of Eden. But God never lost touch with them! God kept doing all kinds of good stuff for them and their descendants, giving them those laws and guidelines that make life workable, and sending them prophets when they went astray. Many of them responded obediently; they didn't act like lost sinners whose minds were darkened by *original sin*. Indeed, some of them seemed to catch a glimpse of the truth about their original identity, and obeyed their *inner light*. Just look at some of the stories that follow.

Enoch who walked so closely with God that God took him home ahead of time (Gen 5:24). Then there's Noah. He wasn't perfect and had some problems with the bottle in his old age. But still, he was "a righteous man and blameless in his generations" and he too walked with God (Gen 6:9). And then there's Abraham. On one occasion, he lied out of fear to protect himself, endangering his wife, Sarah. Nevertheless, he ended up being called the "friend of God" (Jas 2:23). And, of course, there is Moses, who had a temper problem on several occasions. Nonetheless, he was one whom God knew "face to face" (Deut 34:10). Elijah was also imperfect and subject to depression on one occasion, but he was taken home in a special chariot of fire (2 Kgs 2:11). None of them were perfect; however, they let some small shaft of God's light shine, to some degree, in and through their lives. And there may have been many more whose stories were never recorded. It's exactly what we read in the Gospel of John (1:5), "The light shines in the darkness, and the darkness did not overcome it."

So, instead of thinking of ourselves as fallen sinners, let's try thinking of ourselves as imperfect teenagers who can, by God's grace, learn to live gracefully, saying "yes" to God's good will for our lives. None of the great saints of the Bible were perfect. They walked with God, but they made their occasional mistakes and bad decisions. Their spirituality was *a spirituality of imperfection*. When we begin to think of ourselves in this way, we will also begin to read Paul's statements about Adam differently. This will give new depth to his assertion, "for as in Adam all die, so all will be made alive in Christ" (1 Cor 15:22). Just think of that! We are all Adam's children; we are all "in Adam," in his imperfection. But we are also, by God's decision and action, "in Christ." Just as Adam's imperfect condition is universal, so our spiritual condition in Christ is universal. Even though we are all Adam's imperfect children, we are all saved by grace as God's children in Christ!

I have a practical suggestion for how we may want to live in light of what we have learned from the story of what happened in Eden. For starters, instead of using the term *original sin*, I suggest we reflect upon our *perennial sin* of making the kinds of distinctions which God refuses to make. You may recall Peter's sermon in the home of Cornelius in which he begins by saying, "I truly understand that God shows no distinctions" (Acts 10:34). God does not make distinctions between people. For that matter, making distinctions is the principal work of the devil. In Revelation 12:10 the Devil is called "the accuser of our brothers." And the Greek word for "accuser" is *ho kategor* (the categorizer)! So that's the forbidden fruit that is so perennially tempting to God's teenagers! We categorize our brothers and sisters as the bad guys, and withdraw into the isolation of our safe camp as the good guys. If we find ourselves tempted to "circle the wagons," and take our stand unmovably within some safe circle of "true believerism," then let's beware. The voice to which we are listening is *not* the voice of the God who has no favorites. Instead, it is the voice of the categorizer.

If we listen to that voice, we will be eating the fruit that poisons the soul. In the day we eat of it, something in our soul will die.

The antidote for this poison and the resulting soul-sickness was given to us by Jesus when he said, "Love your enemies and pray for those who persecute you, so that you may be children of your Father in heaven; for he makes his sun to rise on the evil and the good, and sends rain on the righteous and the unrighteous" (Matt 5:44–45). This is to be our way of life as those who are God's children, created in God's image and likeness. This, indeed, is the "gospel in a nutshell," the heart of the good news that can save a warring world.

Chapter 5

What Happened
on the Cross?

A cross the conflicting and confusing collection of churches
that call themselves Christian, there is one thing that we
have in common: we all come together around the Lord's table.
The Quakers are an exception to this common practice, understanding the sacraments as inward, spiritual experiences, and so
do not perform outward sacramental ceremonies. For the rest of
us, some kind of celebration of the Lord's Supper takes place in our
worship, but in diverse ways. The high altar of liturgical churches
can seem like a strange, other world to a gathering of traditional,
evangelical, or non-denominational Christians who gather around
a plain table. And then there's the difference of how frequently this
sacrament is celebrated; there is variance even within the same denomination. Some of us celebrate communion weekly, while others only monthly, or even quarterly. Thus, in some churches, Holy
Communion is the main event, the high and holy moment toward
which the worship service moves and comes to a conclusion. But
in other churches in which this sacrament is not a weekly event,
the sermon is often the main event with which the service ends.
Still, with all this diversity, wherever there is some kind of church,

there will be an altar or table around which believers gather to partake of the Lord's Supper.

There is, however, one point upon which we may not agree, even within the same denomination or congregation; we may hear different messages when, within the communion liturgy, we hear the words about the "Lamb of God who takes away the sins of the world" (John 1:29). What do you hear in those words? What does it mean that, as a sacrificial lamb, the body of Christ was broken for you, and that the blood of the Lamb of God was shed for you? My book may not settle that question; however, it may be helpful to consider some thoughts about it.

Proclaiming Jesus as the Lamb of God who takes away the sin of the world may connect *emotionally* with our hearts, even though it may not connect *rationally* with our modern minds. Many of us are moved deeply whenever we hear the words and music of the beloved hymn, "Just As I Am," in which Jesus is presented as a sacrificial lamb "whose blood can cleanse each spot." The very strains of the hymn tune Woodworth can still tug on our heartstrings because of the many memories it evokes of some early Christian experience or evangelistic service in which we responded to an altar call to come forward to receive Christ as Savior. But does the killing of a sacrificial animal have any real meaning for us? It might make some sense for the ancient Hebrews (or other ancient peoples) in whose worship animals were slaughtered to please or appease God. However, for those of us who have never witnessed the killing of a sacrificial animal as a part of our neat and tidy Sunday morning worship, how could such a bloody, brutal action make sense? Would you bring your children to a service in which a bleating, struggling little lamb was killed, right before their eyes?

Perhaps I need to share with you what I call "The Mr. Rogers Test." In an essay that I contributed to a three-volume work, I suggested that we consider the gentle, child-friendly spirit of Fred Rogers when we evaluate any belief or practice. What I meant was that, in formulating our beliefs, we ask the simple question, "Could you tell it to a little child?" When we take our stand on some belief or teaching, we should ask, "How would I teach that to a little kid?" After all, we certainly don't believe that the church's teachings should be rated like our movies as G, PG, R, or NC-17, as though what is truth for grown-ups should be different than what is truth for little ones. Of course, there are Bible stories that we would never share with our children, stories that don't even make sense to us as adults. How do you, for example, make sense of the story about the prophet Elisha (2 Kgs 2:23–24) who, when some little kids made fun of him and called him "baldy" because of his bald head, called down God's wrath upon them so that two she-bears came out of the woods and mauled forty-two of them? What possible sense can we make of such a story (unless it's saying, "Don't mess with us bald old guys!")? There are occasions when we seem to have better judgment than those who decided to include such violent stories in the Bible.

It gets interesting when you apply the Mr. Rogers Test to other doctrines. Could you explain to a child what some people believe about an endless hell of eternal conscious torment? Could you justify to a little child the kind of God who will send their Jewish or Muslim classmates in nursery school into an eternal torture chamber? Or that there are trillions of lost souls who never believed in Jesus who have been screaming in their tortures over the past centuries since they were sent there—and are screaming even today as we sing our lovely hymns of praise on Sunday? If we can't explain such a cruel doctrine to a child, should we believe it ourselves, or preach it to anyone else? This is certainly not a "friendlier Christianity." But you can find that doctrine of eternal, conscious torment in plain English in the mission statements of several popular campus mission organizations that many of our traditional churches may be supporting with their mission dollars.

So, we return to "the Lamb of God who takes away the sin of the world." Did it ever make any sense to believe that God would be moved to mercy by the slaughter of sacrificial animals? In Hebrew Scripture there are prophetic voices that question the salvific value of such worship! Many centuries ago, some Psalmist placed that very question upon God's lips, "Do I eat the flesh of bulls, or drink the blood of goats?" (Ps 50:13). So, we are on firm, scriptural ground with the Hebrew psalmist when we question why God would need to see blood in order to be moved to mercy, or why the "Heavenly Father" of Jesus' teaching would have to kill in order to forgive.

Of course, in that church of my teenage years, we heard numerous sermons in which we were told that God's wrath had to be poured out upon Jesus to effect our salvation. While we did not argue with such recurrent pronouncements, it does not require much reflection to realize that such a notion of substitutionary sacrifice paints a portrait of God as somewhat schizophrenic, or, for that matter, creates a serious imbalance or inconsistency within the Holy Trinity. Just think: we are asked to believe that God, the "heavenly" Father, must find some way to relieve his furious, righteous anger—get the wrath out of his system in order to forgive us. Thus, to resolve his Father's implacable hatred of sinful humanity, Jesus, the loving, friendly Son of God agrees to let his Father take it all out on him. "Don't kill them, Dad; take it out on me." Do we know of any human system of jurisprudence that would allow such substitution? If one of my sons was convicted of a major crime, could I offer to serve his sentence for him? Of course not! So how do we justify such a ridiculous transaction in God's perfect court?

Then too, in this notion of substitutionary sacrifice, Jesus has become the friendly face of God. Indeed, if this is our explanation of the cross, it is saying that what happened on the cross was that Jesus was saving us from God—the God whom Jesus taught us to think of as a loving Father! This does not make sense to us because it is saying that the very God who abhorred the practice of child sacrifice in the Old Testament had now, in the New Testament, resorted to the same practice himself. This simply could not have been what transpired when Jesus was dying upon the cross.

There were, however, other voices that spoke out against such a conflicted image of our Trinitarian God, and offered other possible interpretations of what happened on Calvary. One such voice was that of Peter Abelard (1079–1142), a French theologian whose merciful vision of God was eventually condemned by the official church as heretical. Let's remember, however, that by this time in church history, suggesting that God is amazingly merciful was "bad for business." A fearful God whose wrath must be placated by regular sacramental observances keeps the customers coming back weekly! But Abelard didn't agree, and taught that God is not a cruel tyrant whose wrath was appeased by the death of his Son, but a loving Father whose Son's death revealed God's constant and pre-existing love for all humankind. Jesus did not die on the cross *to change God's mind* toward us, but *to change our minds about God*, and to reveal what had always been God's unchangeable love toward us. The cross was the demonstration of that divine Love which will never give up on us. When Jesus said, "Father, forgive them; for they do not know what they are doing" (Luke 23:34), he was assuring us that all of the hatred poured out upon him by the ruthless powers of the world could not force from him so much as a single word of retaliatory revenge. In the end, "he went down loving."

I think of Calvary as the great "high noon" moment of history, like that moment in the movie *High Noon* when Gary Cooper has a stand-off with the vicious outlaw, Frank Miller. Except that, as all the power, hatred, and cruelty of the world, as embodied in the Roman Empire, finally confronts God's love in Jesus of Nazareth, what happens is that Jesus doesn't "draw," doesn't' even have a gun! It is as though he says, "Go ahead! Make my day! You can't force me to do anything other than forgive and love you eternally!" On that great high noon of history, when the sin of the world tested the love of God, love was the winner! And thus, we sing those grand words Frederick William Faber: "O love of God! O sin of man! In this dread act your strength is tried, And victory remains with love: Jesus, our Lord, is crucified!"

What a celebration of amazing grace takes place when we celebrate Holy Communion with this huge shift of our understanding. The triumph of God's love on the cross has made possible the restoration of all things. Our previous scenario of an eternal, unbridgeable gulf separating heaven and hell is no longer necessary or tenable. If abounding grace, now made even more amazing by the cross, has always been at the secret center of God's heart, then there must, at least, be the everlasting possibility of everyone's return. When it says of the holy city (Rev 21:26) that "Its gates will never be shut by day—and there will be no night there," there must, at least, be the possibility of universal restoration. And is this not the hope we've always sensed in our favorite ancient song, "Surely, goodness and kindness shall *pursue* [the best translation of the Hebrew *radaph*] me all the days of my life" (Ps 23:6)? If God has always been pursuing us in mercy, then we no longer have to pursue converts; God is doing that job. God is engaged in the endless pursuit of every human life.

If this is what we celebrate at the Lord's Table, then I wish I could commune every day because it sends me out into the world in hope. I no longer have to decide who is saved and who is lost; I can now look upon everyone with the hopefulness that was instilled in theologian Christoph Blumhardt by his pastor-theologian father: "My father once wrote to me that I should make it a rule for myself at all times to view everyone as a believer, never to doubt it, and never to talk to a person in any other way." We can now look upon every person, even the most impossible, knowing that Jesus is in hot pursuit of them. Or we can say with Quaker George Fox, "Walk cheerfully over the world, answering that of God in every one." All of this was made manifest by the cross. It did not change God's attitude toward us—which didn't need to be changed. But it made it possible for us to believe in a wonderfully friendly God.

What happened on the cross reminds us that God has no enemies. When Jesus told us to love our enemies, he added, "so that you may be the children of your Father in heaven." Surely, if God tells us to love our enemies, it must mean that God has no enemies. When God commands us to love our enemies, it is because God has already done the same. So, let's get out of our system the notion that God is somehow angry with us from time to time. When you awaken in the morning with some nagging guilt or vague regret over yesterday's failures, get it out of your mind that God must be mad at you. God is never mad at you! There may be times when God is sad *with* us, sympathizing *with* us when we are saddened by our own repetitive failures; however, God is *never* mad at us.

Remember this: God cannot *not* love us. It is impossible for God to be anything other than completely and unalterably in love with us, because God *is* love. This is what was made crystal clear on the cross—don't ever forget it!

So now let's get back to where we left off with the parable of the Prodigal Father and think about the holy family of the Trinity.

Chapter 6

The Great Dinner Dance

The Trinity

Not too many years ago, it would have been thought irreverent to speak of the Holy Trinity in such a light and worldly manner. All of a sudden, however, talking about the Trinity has become trendy. I don't know how many millions of people have attended the movie, *The Shack*, but I do remember that the book upon which it was based (by William Paul Young) was a *New York Times* best seller for thirty-two weeks. Perhaps some of you have already seen the movie or read the book; if you haven't, I hope you will because it provides helpful background for this chapter. We need to do some thinking about this central doctrine of the Christian faith which, according to the Jesuit theologian, Karl Rahner, has had so few practical applications for our daily lives. The Trinity has been more of a theological problem to be solved (though accepted on faith) than a truth to be lived joyfully. How shall we describe "living in the Trinity"?

It is in John's gospel that we notice how God's presence is described sometimes as Father, sometimes as Son, and other times as Spirit. The three persons seem to blend into one another while remaining distinct. Listen to this conversation in the following rendering of *The Message:* Jesus says to Phillip, "Don't you believe that I am in the Father and the Father is in me? (John 14:10). As the conversation continues, Jesus promises he will be coming to them as another kind of presence: "I will talk to the Father, and he'll provide you another Friend so that you will always have someone with you. This Friend is the Spirit of Truth" (John 14:15–16). Jesus enlarges upon the role of this Friend and says, "The Friend, the Holy Spirit whom the Father will send at my request, will make everything plain to you. He will remind you of all the things I have told you. I'm leaving you well and whole . . . I don't leave you the way you're used to being left—feeling abandoned" (John 14:26–27). To those who need neat, clear distinctions, such talk sounds like the talk of mystics—which is exactly what it is. It is depicting God as One whom we experience in three mingling personalities: God above and beyond us as Heavenly Father, God beside us as Jesus Christ, Son of the Father, and God within us as Holy Spirit. There is no competition to be "Number One." It is a circle of self-emptying love and receiving, as in the Christ hymn (Phil 2:6,7) in which Jesus "did not regard equality with God as something to be exploited, but emptied himself." The relationships within the Trinity are like a great, graceful circle dance. Let's look at another scene.

At the end of Chapter 3, we looked at the ending of the parable of the Prodigal Son. I suggested an imaginary Trinitarian ending in which the father, the younger son, and the mother are standing in the outer darkness, pleading with the older brother to join the homecoming banquet. I realize that such a scenario involves taking some imaginative liberties with the text that strict literalists may not enjoy. It also involves some suggestions about the doctrine of the Trinity that may challenge those who do not enjoy new or odd metaphors. To suggest that the Holy Spirit might be a Mother, however, is no more heretical than to suggest that God is a Father. God is beyond all the metaphors by which we seek to understand the divine nature. God is neither male nor female; however, our limited minds need images to help us understand what the love of God may be like, and sometimes it seems that God loves us in the way we have experienced unconditional love from our mother or father.

But now let me carry my scenario to an even wilder extreme. Let us imagine that the older brother has been persuaded, at least, to take a look at the homecoming party, so that all four family members return to the banquet hall. What they see strains the imagination because many more guests have joined in the revelry, not only feasting upon the food, but now dancing with one another—and look at who's dancing! The younger brother's questionable friends from the far country have somehow arrived at the party. The harlots upon whose services he wasted his inheritance, along with his foul-smelling fellow workers at the Gentile hog farm— they're all there—but they now seem to have an inner dignity that has made them part of the family. Unbelievably, they're mingling happily and harmoniously with the older brother's country club, churchgoing friends. (You've probably guessed that the stay-at-home older brother was a traditional, rule-keeping Presbyterian who enjoyed both his church and country club memberships. He was "not the sort to awaken in others the festive spirit.") It is as though a miracle has happened as we see them wining and waltzing, dining and dancing as one family. The circle of self-emptying love that has reunited the younger brother with his family has now infected this wider, diverse circle of humanity around one festive table. Such a scene makes you wonder if this is what Jesus pictured when he told his disciples that history was headed toward the great banquet of the kingdom.

If all of this seems a bit over the top, listen to a revered scholar with whose writings most of you are familiar. I'm sure you'll find it rather odd that C. S. Lewis talked about this great Dance. I call it odd because my guess is that Lewis probably had never danced. Not marrying until late in life, his world was one of male scholars enjoying weekly meetings in a favorite pub, or sitting late in college rooms enjoying what he termed, "beer, and tea, and pipes." And yet he wrote about our Trinitarian God, saying, "in Christianity God is not a static thing—not even a person—but a dynamic, pulsating activity, a life, almost a kind of drama. Almost, if you will not think me irreverent, a kind of dance . . . . The whole dance, or drama, or pattern of this three-Personal life is to be played out in each one of us . . . . [E]ach one of us has got to enter the pattern, take his place in that dance. There is no other way to the happiness for which we were made."

So, as we return to this great homecoming dinner dance, one question remains: did the older brother ever join the party? Well, we'll never know. Even though we've taken liberties with the parable, we can't make guesses about the older brother's decision; we must leave the story unfinished, just as it is in the New Testament. We know that the father, along with the mother and younger brother, will never give up on him, ever hoping for his return to the family. Still, we don't know. Did he sit sulking as a wallflower on the edge of the dance floor? Was he even more frustrated by the change in behavior of his church and country club friends who were now socializing with the tacky visitors from the far country? Does his reluctance give us a picture of the hell of endless love in which some souls will be imprisoned when they discover that there's no place else to go, no other destination for our souls other than life in the presence of our loving God? How utterly miserable it would be if one refused to dance to the music of heaven in the world to come!

And does that explain why some people, even today in this present world, are so strangely miserable? Have you ever noticed how miserable some people are, even though they are filling their lives with all kinds of stuff that, supposedly, would make them happy? The more they accumulate more cars and clothes, more second and third vacation homes, and take more trips around the world—nothing seems to fill a hole at the center of their souls. Nothing can give them joy, because they're trying to drown out the sound of that music that is summoning them to dance.

But there is no escaping the great Dance; we cannot leave the dance floor. When Jesus became human, lived, died, rose again, and ascended to the heavenly presence, we were all carried with him into the dance hall. It is an accomplished fact; "It is finished" (John 19:30), just as Jesus said. Like it or not, we're members of a dancing family; sooner or later, we'll either learn to dance or live in misery on the sidelines. This is what is going on right now. This is the great flowing rhythm of Trinitarian life in which we will all, sooner or later, either flow homeward happily, or forever flail against the irresistible current. Why not surrender now? It's so simple. The Shakers understood this mystery.

> 'Tis the gift to be simple, 'tis the gift to be free, 'Tis the gift to come down where we ought to be. And when we find ourselves in the place just right, 'Twill be in the valley of love and delight.

> When true simplicity is gained, To bow and to bend we shan't be ashamed, To turn, turn will be our delight, Till by turning, turning we come 'round right.

"But wait! All this dancing is too much for me," some older reader says. "Just the thought of such dancing tires me out." I hear you. At age eighty-nine, and with poor balance, I have to sit on the sidelines at family wedding receptions. Is there no other imagery that will make Trinity living meaningful for me? Yes, there is, because our Trinitarian God has a habit of showing up at the family table. Sometimes, the Bible pictures the banquet as a smaller, intimate, family meal.

In Genesis (18:1–8), as Abraham sits in the door of his tent in the heat of the day, three men appear. In the presence of the three, Abraham sees one divine presence, and addresses them as "My Lord." In this early picture of God's "family-like" nature, Abraham receives them with hospitality and, with Sarah's cookery, serves them dinner. The divine visitors have made themselves at home at Abraham's table.

It will happen again, but with a slight difference, in the lovely story about the evening of the first Easter when the risen Jesus (who is one with the Father, and who becomes visibly present by the Spirit) suddenly appears along the road to Emmaus. He will make himself at home and "take over" the role of host in the home of Cleopas (Luke 24:30). Talk about family! This God simply arrives uninvited at the family table.

Better yet, in a reversal of the Abraham story in which Abraham and Sarah are the hosts, we see another scene by the shores of the Sea of Tiberias (John 21:1–14). Seven of the disciples, assuming that Jesus has died, have returned to where it all began; they have returned to their trade as fishermen. After a long, fishless night, through the early morning fog they catch the appetizing aroma of broiling fish, and see the dim outline of a stranger on the shore. It is the risen Jesus, and he has taken on the lowly task of cooking breakfast for his friends.

I wonder if these scenes are all telling us that, even if our dancing days on earth are done, there's always a Friend who shows up for dinner. There's a passage in one of Rilke's *Letters on Cezanne* that has fascinated me for several decades. I've never been sure why, but now I think I know. He writes about walking past little secondhand bookstores on the rue de Seine, fascinated by the fact that, although they seem to do no business, the owners sit near the front window, reading a book, seemingly unconcerned. They apparently have "not a thought about tomorrow, no worrying about success, a dog sitting in front of them, good-natured, or a cat that makes the stillness around them even greater by brushing along the rows of books as if to wipe the names off their backs." And then he writes, "sometimes I dream of buying a full shop window like that and sitting down behind it with a dog for twenty years. In the evening there would be light in the back room, the front would be dark, and we would be sitting in the back together, the three of us, eating; I've noticed how, when you look in from the street, it always looks like a Last Supper, so great and solemn through the dark room."

Who are "the three of us" to whom he refers? I've never tried to find out what Rilke meant, but I've wondered if, whenever we dine, some divine presence is always trying to be at home with us, almost as though this Someone is a member of the family—or as though we're a part of some larger family.

Chapter 7

I Like You Just the Way You Are

In my years at the Shadyside Church of Pittsburgh, Fred Rogers, creator of *Mister Rogers' Neighborhood*, became a good friend. We discovered that we were born in same month and year, March of 1928, and that we had the same initials, F. M. R. (Fred McFeely Rogers, and Frederick Morgan Roberts). Because of that, Fred would always remember my birthday. As I write these words, I'm looking at my bookcase where I keep one of those birthday cards. Fred is smiling, wearing his traditional red, zipper-front sweater and sneakers. Over the photo are the words, "I like you just the way you are." The amazing thing about those words is that they were not just birthday greetings for a few friends, but words that expressed how Fred felt about every person. For that matter, Fred believed that those words expressed how God feels about every person on the face of the earth. Fred's "theology" (Fred was a theological seminary graduate and an ordained Presbyterian minister) focused principally upon God's universal grace and love. If that requires some stretching of your mind, begin by thinking about it on a smaller scale. Just reflect upon Fred's words as an expression of how God always thinks about you. God likes you just the way you are!

Well, that's not always easy to believe; in fact, I find it very difficult because I often don't like myself "just the way I am." Besides that, we all know a few people who always *do* like themselves the way they are, and it's not much fun being around them. Fred certainly wasn't talking about people like that, the kind whose smug satisfaction makes them snobbish and boorish! So maybe Fred meant something deeper. Which *me* did Fred like "just the way" I am? Think of it this way: There's a *surface me* that you see, and then there's an invisible *real me* down under all the surface stuff.

The *me* you see on the surface consists of lots of stuff. I have a title, "Reverend," conferred upon me by my denomination, upon completion of certain exams. Some of you have similar titles: Doctor, President, Professor, or some other title, and we may take those titles more or less seriously. (I've never liked being called Reverend; it sounds like I'm somehow holier than ordinary folks.) In addition to my title, there's all the other stuff that people see. I dress in a certain way. I wear a necktie on Sunday because, even though my parents weren't churchgoers, when we went to my grandmother's house for Sunday dinner, we all wore neckties. So, it's just a habit of doing what I was taught; it doesn't make me special. Other men wear neckties because of the business in which they're employed, just as still other men wear work shoes and hard hats for their work. And then we have our cars, plain or fancy, and our houses, filled with both necessary and unnecessary possessions. Some of it may be cosmetic so we can "look the part," maintain a certain image, while other possessions, like our toys, may not be necessary—it's just stuff we enjoy and can afford to accumulate. All of this is what people see when they see the *surface me* or the *surface you*.

A huge amount of our time on earth must be spent managing this "mountain." From the moment we get up in the morning until bedtime, we have to think about how we look to others, what we'll prepare for dinner, what things we need to buy, what deadlines we must meet—all of this activity just to tend to the surface of our life. Amid such busy maintenance, most of us forget that most people on the face of the earth must spend their day just finding something (or anything) to eat, some leftover piece of clothing to wear, or some roof over their head. The deprived life of millions doesn't mean that our life on the surface is bad, but it might serve as a reminder that, finally, our surface life, affluent or deprived, is going to come to an end. And this realization just might get us thinking about some other, deeper life—maybe the deeper life about which Fred Rogers was thinking.

This is where we need to think about Jesus, the Christ, because what we see in him, is the pattern of that deeper life of which Fred was speaking. Many people think that Christ was Jesus' last name (as though he was the son of Mary Christ!). It's not that way at all. When we speak of Jesus, the Christ, we mean that the cosmic Christ, God's universal presence in every human life, became fully and perfectly incarnate, completely enfleshed in the life of Jesus of Nazareth. When we use the term *Christ*, we're referring to the presence of God that has always been present in every life since creation. But when God decided that the time was right, God's Son, the second person of the Trinity, came to earth in the human life of Jesus of Nazareth. In Jesus' ordinary life on this earth, God was showing us what always was, and *still is* meant to be the reality for every life. From before the creation of the world, this is the quality of real life God intended for all of us. Of course, except for a few saintly souls who "got the point," we mostly forgot our identity as God's children. Finally, however, God descended to earth and lived in an ordinary body like ours to show us what we have always been meant to be.

Better yet, Jesus is more than a pattern to be imitated; God is secretly at work in every life, seeking to form the eternal Christ-life in us. You may not be aware of it, but God is at work in your life, day and night, laboring patiently to restore and remake you into the authentic child of God you're meant to be. Paul said something like that once when he was writing to the Ephesians, "For we are his workmanship, created in Christ Jesus for good works" (2:10). The Greek word for workmanship, *poema*, is the one from which we get our word "poetry." We are the living poetry that God is trying to write into the world, God's fine artistry, created to beautify the world. In fact, we are being carried along with Jesus, the Christ, in his eternal journey. We are dying with him, rising with him, and ascending with him into God's heavenly presence. Paul even says that our spiritual identity matches that of Christ. Writing to the Colossians, he says, "you have died, and your life is hidden with Christ in God" (3:3). This is what is going on in every human life!

I can hear some folks saying, "Slow down now. This is too much!" So, let me make it clear that I am *not* saying that, sooner or later, the entire world will embrace Christianity. To experience Christ is not the same as embracing Christianity. To say, with Paul, that "in Christ God was reconciling the world to himself" (2 Cor 5:19) is *not* to say that, eventually, all will become members of the Christian church. But it is to say that Jesus' cosmic role as the Christ is working in every life at a deeper level than their religious faith—even if they deny having a religious identity! God did not enter our world to start a new religion, but to invade the life of every person with the divine presence, whatever their surface religious affiliation may be. When you understand this important distinction, then you can see why Fred Rogers can say, "I like you just the way you are." I can like everyone just the way they are because, at some deeper level, I know that God's secret work is going on at all times. That is why I said at the beginning of this book that I didn't need to fix anyone; God is already at work fixing them in ways that only God knows. What a relief it is to know that I am not called to a ministry of "fixing." Instead, I can enjoy living with the beautiful mystery of God's working presence in every life. It's almost like a second conversion to arrive at this realization.

That was the eye-opening conversion experienced by Thomas Merton when he realized that his calling as a Trappist monk could not separate him from the rest of God's family. A historical marker at the corner of Fourth and Walnut Streets in downtown Louisville indicates the spot where Merton had his encounter with this universal spiritual reality. The marker mentions how Merton realized that God's presence at the center of every human life made him aware that we are all "shining like the sun" because of the divine presence. Just to be near the secret beauty of any human life is to be near to God, so that the gate of Heaven is everywhere.

It was Merton's *Mister Rogers* moment of realizing that God likes all of us just the way we are, and that such a love is expressed every day in nature as God "makes his sun rise on the evil and on the good, and sends rain on the righteous and on the unrighteous" (Matt 5:44–45). The saintly Anglican missionary to India, Charles F. Andrews, who buried himself so completely in lowly service as to be known as the "friend of the poor," wrote at the end of his life, "What I have been seeking to learn all these years, through storm and stress, goes right back to the character of God himself as it is revealed to us by Christ. It means that God, our Heavenly Father, whose nature and character Christ came to teach us, is truly the Father of all mankind and not of any single race or sect of creed. He is no tribal God. He favours no denomination. He is bound up with no race. He loves mankind. His mercy is over all his works and His goodness is made known to all the children of men. He is no respecter of persons, and even those who outwardly appear to deny Him are still His children, embraced in the arms of His love."

I realize that I'm running ahead of some of you. As lovely as such universal idealism may seem in writing, it is difficult for us to think of all the impossible, violent, and dangerous people in the world, and then imagine saying to them, "I like you just the way you are." That *is* a bit too much! Except for the fact that the early Christians did that very thing. What undermined the power of the Roman Empire was that those early Christians represented another larger empire, the kingdom (Empire) of God. They were "endlessly, foolishly, and incredibly merciful" to the point of loving the very enemies who were feeding them to the lions. In obedience to the command of Jesus (Matt 5:44), they went to their death praying for their persecutors. They did that because of their belief that the cosmic Christ was present in every human life. They believed in the unrealized presence of Christ in every life, as though there's a tiny candle of God's light awaiting discovery in one of the unexplored rooms in the house of every heart. They could love their enemies because they knew that Christ was somehow present, awaiting

gnition in every life. The Christ in them caught a tiny glimpse
he Christ hidden in the hearts of their enemies. That's one aspect of the Lord's Prayer that we have somehow lost. When the
first Christians prayed, "Thy kingdom come" they were including
everyone in their understanding of what they defined as a larger
inclusive, worldwide family of God, even their enemies. In a profound sense, Jesus represented the end of religion, that is, religion
as consisting of separate families of faith who consider themselves
the real thing, the true faith, the genuine insiders. Instead, Jesus
was inaugurating one world family of faith. In this larger empire of
faith, all are citizens, all are saved, all are beloved children of God.

Such a larger, broader kingdom of God seems to frustrate
many Christians who have withdrawn into their own tight and
tiny circles, thinking of *their* church as the one true church. But
it was not that way in the early centuries. Augustine wrote, "The
church consists of the communion of the whole world." Such
larger thinking has somehow been forgotten by the separate tribal
groups that now think of themselves as possessing the "only true
faith." According to their narrow way of thinking, being baptized
in the right church, believing the right doctrines, or practicing the
right rituals—as defined by *their* church—identify them as God's
thoroughbreds. Some of these purebreds classify other religious
beliefs as either mongrel, or even devilish. Such tribalism was un-
thinkable to those early church fathers who described the church
with the words, "*Ubi Christus, ibi ecclesia*," meaning, "Wherever
Christ is, there is the church." It is into such larger, cosmic thinking that we are invited—and it is, indeed, like a second Damascus
road experience when we are suddenly jerked out of our cloistered
clannishness into the realization that God's invasion of the world
in Christ has refuted such holy haughtiness. God's worldwide
kingdom of love and justice is where all of history is moving. God
likes all of us, just as we are!

Chapter 8

Jesus,
the Extraordinary Ordinary

Because of what we have said in the previous chapter about Jesus, the Christ, as the pattern for every human life, we must pause now and do some rethinking about the ordinary life of Jesus of Nazareth. We don't usually think about the life of Jesus as ordinary. To get going on this new way of thinking about Jesus let's pretend that it's Christmas and we're listening to the lectionary text called the gospel for Christmas Day (John 1:1–14). In *The Message*, Eugene Peterson renders verse 14 as follows: "The Word became flesh and moved into the neighborhood." This wording gives us an important clue about what Jesus looked like when he walked upon our earth. The neighborhood in which someone begins their life can tell us some important things about the person and, in this case, we must begin by realizing that Jesus' hometown, Nazareth, wasn't much of a neighborhood. "Can anything good come out of Nazareth?" (John 1:46) was the response of Nathanael when he was about to be introduced to Jesus for the first time. Evidently, Nazareth was something much less than a classy neighborhood. However, take a look at that larger neighborhood of the Roman Empire in which the Son of the Father landed.

It was a cruel neighborhood. Somewhere between 30 to 40 percent of the population of Italy lived in slavery, half of whom were owned by 1.5 percent of the population. In Jesus' native Galilee, a lesser percentage lived in slavery, but the general population lived in conditions worse than slavery. Their country was occupied by the armies of Rome, and thus was no longer their own. For that matter, it's important to remember that every word of the New Testament was written under Roman occupation. People like Jesus' family lived under brutal, oppressive taxation from which there was no escape. To help us understand the harsh circumstances in which Jesus' family lived, let's realize that living under Roman occupation would have been worse than living in a world controlled by ISIS. Rebellion was dealt with by crucifixion. The kind of cross upon which Jesus died was just one of many thousands upon which troublemakers, those who rebelled against Rome, suffered a torturous death—not a scenic death upon a hillside, as Calvary is often romantically rendered, but a cross along any public road, where the body was left hanging until it was crawling with insects or torn away by wild dogs before being tossed into a limed pit. Long before his own crucifixion, Jesus would have seen such awful reminders about the consequences of disturbing the Roman peace, if one could call such suppression "peace."

In such a world, Jesus was born into a poor family in which his father was a *tekton*, not a high-end carpenter, but something like a construction worker, a member of a lower class of landless people, a class lower than the peasants who still had the minimal dignity of owning a small piece of land. Worse yet, with 95 to 97 percent of the Jewish population being illiterate in those times, the probability of either Mary or Joseph being able to read is highly unlikely. So, let's never get the picture of Jesus, Mary, and Joseph sitting down at night to read a passage from their Scofield Reference Bible because people in Jesus' day didn't have "family Bibles," and expensive Torah scrolls were for synagogues—and even if they had one, there is little probability that they could have read it. Do you see where I'm going? Jesus was born into a very poor, illiterate family. He was very ordinary, very common.

And yet many, if not most, Christians picture Jesus as someone other than an ordinary human being. Instead, they picture him as someone like Superman, who comes down to earth from another planet called heaven. He dresses like other people, but underneath his robe, like Clark Kent, "mild-mannered reporter of the *Daily Planet*," he always wears his Superman outfit, ready to jump off tall buildings and do all sorts of miraculous stuff. He even allows his enemies to kill him, just to prove that he can pull off the big miracle of rising from the dead, after which he returns to planet heaven, promising those who believe in him that he'll take them there to live with him forever, leaving behind those who don't believe to suffer in hell forever. That's the super Jesus in which most Christians believe, a Jesus who engaged in a temporary thirty-three–year masquerade, a Jesus who really wasn't one of us. But that is the very kind of superhuman Jesus that the real Jesus rejected when he was tempted by Satan, who urged him to become such a worldly, spectacular superhuman. And, of course, such a super Jesus is pure heresy, because Scripture insists that the Word become flesh, a genuine flesh and blood human being like the rest of us. Jesus was ordinary!

We also need to note that Jesus was not a highly educated person. There has been, of course, extensive scholarly debate about the literacy of Jesus, ranging all the way from those who insist that he was literate to those who contend that he was not. While we cannot take time to enter into this debate, there is a moderate middle ground of opinion that suggests that, while Jesus did not possess the official literacy of the scribal class, he had somehow acquired a depth of understanding about some portions of Hebrew Scripture. Jesus' grasp of Scripture somehow convinced some Jewish authorities, along with the common people, that his teaching had an inner authority that matched or exceeded that of the official scribal scholars. How he acquired this knowledge of Scripture we do not know. However, what is certain is that he could not, given the social circumstances of his family, have had the time or opportunity to have received an advanced education. He possessed no earned degrees. For that matter, seeing him within the context of first-century Palestine, Jesus knew less about the world than the sixth-grade students whom I tutor weekly. My students know more about the world's history, geography, and natural science than Jesus could ever have known. There was a limited "neighborhood of knowledge" into which Jesus was born and by which he was bound, just as we are all confined by the limitations of knowledge of our own time. None of us can possess the yet-discovered knowledge that will not be known until centuries after the time of our death. To make Jesus a superhuman exception to his own cultural heritage is to deny that he truly became one of us.

But even when we insist that Jesus was an ordinary human being, we must also insist that he represents what I shall term "God's extraordinary ordinary." He knew something that an advanced education cannot give us. He knew how to open his ordinary life in an extraordinary manner to the will of God. While Jesus did not possess the kind of knowledge acquired by a higher education, what he did possess was that deeper wisdom that can be acquired only by opening our hearts fully to the will of God. And that is why the ordinary life of Jesus is so extraordinary. Because he lived every moment of his life saying, "Thy will be done," his ordinariness is so overwhelming, his simplicity is so shattering, and his plainness so piercing. Try thinking about Jesus' deeper wisdom by the following example.

How often has a bright young college graduate returned to his rural hometown, gone to visit his saintly, uneducated grandmother who, in a tiny home, lives a life of poverty and prayer—and has come away realizing that his grandmother somehow knows more about life than he does! Saintliness does not depend upon sophistication; holiness needs no PhD. Now magnify such plain piety, such shattering simplicity, to the highest possible degree and you have Jesus, the ordinary man who opened his life fully to the presence and will of his heavenly Father. Into such a life—into God's extraordinary ordinary—we are invited. The Son of God came into our world to show us who we really are, who we really were always meant to be, to show us our true selves, the "child-of-God selves" we really are down under all our phony, pretentious self-images. When you are looking at the life of Jesus, you're seeing what human life is meant to be. And remember, he lived his extraordinary life in a body and mind like yours! He didn't have any special equipment. You have all that you need to follow his kind of life!

So, just begin by thinking of the many things that Jesus was never able to do within the limited span of his short life. He never had a chance to play a musical instrument; but perhaps you are one of those given that gift for God's glory. He never had the opportunity to be a parent; so you can be a mom or dad who live out all the possibilities of Christlike parenthood. And if you're saying that it's too late for you to be a part of this exciting story, remember that Jesus never had a chance to grow old, so you can display what it means when the Christ-life adorns the sunset glory of old age.

You don't need anything other than your ordinary humanity to be part of the ongoing story of Jesus. You don't need to go back to school. You don't need a facelift or a better body. Jesus lived a life filled with God's presence in a body just like yours. You don't need a new vehicle to travel the road of the Christ-life; any old vehicle will do. Just as you are, you can do the one and only thing for which you were born. You can say "yes" to the Christ-life and let God's presence fill your life. The story goes on, and you are invited to be some essential part of that story, beginning today. There is no need to wait another moment. You can open your life to all the possibilities for which you were born before you finish reading this chapter! In the words of that contemporary of Jesus, Rabbi Hillel, "If not now, when?" And if you say "yes" today, you'll begin seeing something new about everyone else, because everyone else in the entire world is a child of God, carrying the hidden presence of the cosmic Christ somewhere in their heart, awaiting recognition. You'll begin to realize that the story of Jesus can continue to be told in many lives today.

At the very end of the Gospel of John (21:25) we read, "But there are also many other things that Jesus did; if every one of them were written down, I suppose that the world itself could not contain the books that would be written." Could that verse be telling us that, in each of our lives, another new book about Jesus could be written, that we are the new books about Jesus that God is still seeking to publish? What an amazing thought, that your life can be a new version of the story of Jesus! Try living through every day, working on today's chapter, revising, rewriting, making your life one of the greatest stories ever told. And be on the lookout for others in whose lives the same great story is being retold!

Chapter 9

What About Evangelism and Being Born Again?

During a lecture I was delivering several years ago, a "born again" believer felt that he had to ask a question, even though it had no connection with the subject of my lecture. His question was actually an assertion, "Do you agree that the most important mission of the church is that of getting people to accept Jesus Christ as their personal savior?" I responded with a question, "What is the scriptural basis for your assertion?" Just as I might have anticipated, he quoted John 3:7 from his King James Bible, "Ye must be born again."

Without landing too hard so as to embarrass him publicly, I responded briefly that the pronoun (ye) in Jesus' words to Nicodemus is plural. Jesus is *not* saying to Nicodemus that he must be personally born again. Instead, Jesus is addressing the larger community of which Nicodemus is a representative, saying, "You must all be born from above." Of course, we do not possess a verbatim record of the conversation that took place between Jesus and Nicodemus. That conversation would have been conducted in Aramaic, the common language of Jesus' day. What we have in John 3 is an interpretation for a later audience for whom Greek was the common language. But what that passage in Greek is telling us is that

vas a confusion of terms going on in this conversation sur-
⌐ounding an important word. Jesus was talking about being born
"from above" (*anothen*), but the same word can mean "again" or
"anew," and Nicodemus hears it in that way as he asks, "How can a
man be born when he is old?" Note the confusion: Jesus is talking
about being born "from above," but Nicodemus hears him talking about being "born again." Jesus was *not* the original source of
"born-again Christianity." Nicodemus gets the credit for that term.

So, Jesus gets more specific and explains to Nicodemus that
one must be born of the Spirit. "What is born of the flesh is flesh,
and what is born of the Spirit is spirit" (John 3:6). Nicodemus is
speaking as the representative of a Jewish community that does
not understand the spirituality of Jesus' message. To comprehend
what's happening in this famously misunderstood interchange, we
need to understand the larger context of the Gospel of John.

In the years following Jesus' ministry, the Jews in Palestine
were divided into different parties. There were different interpretations of what it meant to be Jewish, but there was no single
"correct" definition of who was and who was not the real item,
even though there was disagreement and competition between the
various parties. There were groups such as the Essenes who lived
in a monastic community near the Dead Sea. And then there were
the Sadducees who were closely aligned with the Jerusalem priest-
hood. Another well-known group was the Pharisees, about whom
we hear much during Jesus' ministry. What we fail to understand
is that the first Christians were another separate party within this
mix. However, they were not called Christians. This designation
came much later, not until twenty-five to thirty years after Jesus'
ministry, and then it was applied to non-Jewish followers of Jesus
outside Palestine. Before the Gospel of John was written, the first
generation of Jews who believed in Jesus had no special designation; they were just one Jewish party who happened to be followers
of Jesus of Nazareth. These early Jewish followers of Jesus in Palestine didn't "go to church on Sunday" as we assume. They didn't
build separate church buildings in which to worship. Instead, they
continued to do what they had always done; they kept the Jewish

Sabbath and coexisted with other Jews. An outsider would have seen little difference between these Nazarenes (as they later came to be called) and other faithful Jews. However, all of this changed after the destruction of the Temple in 70 CE.

To describe what happened briefly, let us say that there was a tightening of the definition of what it meant to be Jewish, and the new narrower view of Jewish orthodoxy was one that excluded the Jewish followers of Jesus, the Nazarenes. It was in this historical context that the Gospel of John was written. The new Jewish orthodoxy was one that threatened the Nazarenes with expulsion from the synagogues (brief references to which we can see in the Gospel of John), and this was particularly painful because, with the Temple gone forever, their worship now took place in the synagogue. The Nazarenes no longer had a place where they were welcomed to worship. Because of this, we notice in the Gospel of John that there is a note of hostility toward "the Jews," an oft-repeated phrase in this fourth Gospel. This is not, however, a reference to our Jewish friends and neighbors nowadays. "The Jews" in John refers to the Jewish authorities, the enemies of Jesus, who had now rejected the Jewish followers of Jesus as no longer being truly Jewish.

All of this means that we must read the Gospel of John within the context of that ancient conflict, a conflict between different groups of Jews, and *not* a prescription for evangelism and the conversion of participants of the other world religions in our world today. The Gospel of John is not talking about evangelism in today's world. So, when we read in John 14:6 that Jesus is the "way," Jesus is not offering a theological strategy for evangelism. The mistreated Nazarenes of that day are being assured that Jesus is truly the "way" to be a faithful Jew, an authentic way to live faithfully and obediently as children of God's covenant with Israel. This does not mean that our Jewish friends today are excluded from that ancient covenant, but it does means that, as Christians, *we* are included, that we too are children of Abraham. So, when Jesus talks with Nicodemus, his conversation is a loving invitation to those Jewish authorities (represented symbolically by Nicodemus) who were excluding the Nazarenes, an invitation to discover the new life in the Spirit that Jesus' life, death, and resurrection has made possible. That's the real heart of the gospel that is being offered to all of us in this often misunderstood fourth Gospel. But does this mean that centuries of world missionary effort, based largely upon the misunderstanding of these texts in John 3 and 14, was misdirected and "off course"?

What we have just discussed about the true meaning of being born of the Spirit and understanding Jesus as the Way could be heard as a criticism of the many faithful missionaries who made extraordinary sacrifices in carrying the gospel to nations of the world in the effort to "save lost souls." Our hymnals still contain favorite hymns that remind us of that heroic era of missionary endeavor. Many of us can still sing from memory, "O Zion, haste, thy mission high fulfilling, to tell to all the world that God is light, that He who made all nations is not willing one soul should perish, lost in shades of night." Would anyone dare to assert that this major emphasis of nearly every Christian denomination was in vain? Of course not! We say to all such brave soldiers of the cross, "Your labor is not in vain in the Lord" (1 Cor 15:58). After all, none of us can ever measure the success of our efforts to proclaim the good news, whether here on the "home" mission field or abroad on the "foreign" mission field.

Just consider some of the tangible results of the church's world mission endeavor. Many of the hospitals and schools in what were called "heathen" lands were the result of Christian missionary work. Atheists who deride zealous evangelism have few, if any, monuments of practical humanitarian accomplishment to which they can point. Unbelief has done little to make the world a better place. It is true that many mission hospitals and schools were established as a way of attracting potential converts to the faith. The goal in view was more than the healing of the body or the enlightening of the mind; the final aim was the salvation of the eternal soul. But, unknown to those missionaries, a deeper healing and enlightenment was often taking place. After all, we never know what is happening in the depths of any life. We've never had an accurate instrument for measuring inner spiritual success. What am I saying?

There were missionaries in many countries, especially in Muslim lands, who spent many years of service without winning a single convert. But how would we possibly know what really happened to those who did not "change their religion" by becoming proselytes to Christian belief? We know that some who did not "buy" the Christian message were still grateful for the benefits of medical missions. Because of what they had received, they studied medicine in the countries from which the missionaries had come and, thereafter, returned to their homeland to practice medicine among their people. Was not their healing work, even if not done theologically in the name of Jesus, nonetheless the genuine work of Jesus? The missionary enterprise may not have turned out "according to plan," but the work of Christ was continued in a way that the missionaries might never have imagined. The work of the cosmic Christ, whose presence is not confined to any church or belief system, can be done by those who know him by some other name. Wherever persons of good faith (or no faith) do the work of healing, whether they realize it or not, it is still true that, "The healing of His seamless dress is by our beds of pain; we touch him in life's throng and press, and we are whole again."

Chapter 10

The Evidence
for the Empty Tomb

This chapter's title is meant to be a bit misleading; it's about the resurrection of Jesus, but not in the sense you may be anticipating. Let's start, however, by recognizing that Christians have differing interpretations of what happened on the first Easter. Many have always taken the Easter stories in the Gospels as a matter of history, despite the ways in which the accounts seem to disagree on certain details. Faced with those discrepancies in the Gospel accounts, we can call attention to the fact that eyewitnesses to the same traffic accident often differ. What remains is that they all saw it happen; they just describe it with different words and images. However, there are other, sincere followers of Jesus who interpret the Easter event in entirely different ways, some in a radically different way.

Some scholars believe that it took time for Easter to happen; that it had to evolve gradually in the hearts and minds of Jesus' followers. It is as though, in the weeks and months after his death, they sensed his living presence, somewhat in the way we may feel that our own recently deceased loved ones are somehow still present with us. Building upon this, according to these scholars, they came to use the language of resurrection to describe this new sense of a living presence, and proceeded to make up stories about an empty tomb and other appearances of the risen Jesus. There are, however, some practical problems with this interpretation of the story of the empty tomb as a gradually developed memory. And the big practical problem is that the early Christians began living in a radically different manner that such gradually developed memories could not conceivably inspire. One does not live the way they lived upon the basis of stories that have been manufactured.

The first shocking change in their behavior was that private property was abolished. They began sharing their possessions with one another, especially with the poor. After the Day of Pentecost, "All who believed were together and had all things in common; they would sell their possessions and goods and distribute the proceeds to all, as they had need" (Acts 2:45). And this was not just a "first, fine careless rapture" of early zeal that would fade away. Much later in the first century, when the pastoral letters to Timothy were written, the daily feeding of widows and orphans was still happening. Even those who were enemies of the early church call attention to this radical, communal practice. For that matter, when Rome began arresting and persecuting the early Christians, it was easy to find them because of these gatherings in which the poor were being fed. The first strong evidence for the reality of the empty tomb was this new communal way of life. The economically transformed lives of the first Christians constituted strong proof that something of shattering significance had happened on that first Easter morn. People do not liquidate their resources and distribute them to the poor on the basis of a memory. Only an empty tomb could inspire such behavior. What this means is that the empty tomb is much more than an event, the historicity of which we are asked to accept; it is the summons to an entirely new way of living. The real proof of the empty tomb is our way of life!

And yet who could ever look at the lifestyle of the average Christian in our day and deduce from its simplicity and sacrifice that something really mind-blowing happened on the first Easter? Who would ever guess nowadays today that we are genuine "Easter people"? Few, if any, church members connect Easter with bject of how they spend their money. Have you ever heard a sermon about the stewardship of your money on Easter Sunday? How inappropriate that would seem to the crowd of "one-timers" who gather for their annual Easter visit. That's the kind of sermon we expect to hear about in November on what we call Stewardship Sunday, when we are asked to make our annual pledge of support to the church's ministry and mission. On Easter, however, we expect to hear a comforting sermon about everlasting life after death, or about future reunion with loved ones. But that was not the first response of the early Christians; they recognized immediately that the resurrection had something to do with their checkbook. Such a thought would spoil Easter for many of us!

To see how far we've come from the lifestyle of the early Christians consider the results of an experiment I conducted in one of my churches. After consultation with the county department of public welfare, I calculated what the total income of the congregation would be if every family in the church was so poor as to be living upon public assistance. (This particular church, by the way, was an affluent congregation by most standards. Several families were from "old money," while many others had made it on their own in their professions or in the corporate world.) Still, despite the prosperity of the members, raising the annual budget was always a struggle. So, my question was: what would it be like if, in contrast to our affluence, our church was a "welfare church," with all the members struggling to make ends meet—and what if, at that subsistence level, such folks on welfare still took their faith seriously and were tithers? Well then, we would have a problem indeed, but not the problem you might think. The financial problem with which the officers of the church would be confronted would be that we'd be receiving so much extra money that we'd have to start giving it away! A tithing "welfare church" would receive three times the amount of money that was being contributed by the actual affluent church! And I suspect that the results of my experiment would probably hold true for most congregations. Granted such facts, how would anyone ever know that we are the descendants of those first Christians who really believed in and lived by the reality of the empty tomb?

But wait! It gets more demanding, because the reality of the empty tomb persuaded the early Christians to believe and obey the command of Jesus to "love your enemies and pray for those who persecute you" (Matt 5:44). They understood that commandment, without exception, to be their new way of life. And, of course, they were persecuted because the lordship of Christ made it impossible for them to acknowledge the lordship of the Caesar. The kingdom (empire) of God had definitively arrived in the life, death, and resurrection of Jesus. This was their new citizenship and, as members of this rival empire, they were viewed as subversives. The tortures they endured are sickening to describe, and become even more sickening when we realize that such nightmarish persecutions were staged as entertainment for the crowds who gathered to enjoy such fiendish brutalities.

Eusebius tells of how four Christians were tortured in the year 177. "Maturus, Sanctus, Blandina, and Attalus were taken to the wild beasts in the amphitheater, to give the pagan crowd which was gathered there a public spectacle of inhumanity . . . . [T]hey were dragged around and mauled by the wild beasts. Everything the raving, yelling mob wanted, now from this side, now from that, they endured." After that, they were placed upon a red-hot iron chair "which roasted their bodies so that the fumes rose up . . . . When they were still found alive in spite of the terrible and prolonged torture, they were finally killed. Blandina was hung on a post, delivered up to the wild beasts for food. Hung up like this in the shape of a cross, she could be seen from afar, and through her ardent prayers . . . it was shown to all who believe in Him that everyone who suffers for the glory of Christ is always in fellowship with the living God." Such obedience to the command of Jesus carried the teaching of non-violence to an almost unimaginable level, but what else could Jesus have meant when he taught us to love our enemies and pray for them even when they are persecuting us?

Of course, such radical obedience was all too much. Following the era of the Emperor Constantine, under whose rule

Christianity was legalized, the church gradually became wealthy, and also became violent, killing those who opposed it. Could that be why there is no mention of such extreme discipleship in the Nicene Creed, which is the product of that era? Thus, one can become a member of the church today, recite the Creed faithfully every Sunday, and never be reminded of the fact that Christians once renounced their wealth to live sacrificial, communal lives, and that they also took the words of Jesus about loving their enemies seriously and literally. However, a faithful few have never forgotten what it once meant to follow the Risen Christ.

In Holland in 1569, a Mennonite named Dirk Willems was being pursued by a heretic hunter employed by the "true church." The penalty for the practice of Mennonite pacifism was death. However, as the chase crossed a frozen body of water, the ice gave way under the hunter so that he fell into the freezing water, his drowning death assured. Dirk Willems faced a decision. Was he prepared to believe that his enemy was a child of God, deserving of love and rescue? So, Dirk, the heretic, turned back, reached out to his hunter, saving his life, after which the hunter did his duty, and arrested the heretic. Dirk Willems was thereafter tried, sentenced, and burned at the stake over a "lingering fire." And all of this was done in the name of Jesus by sincere Christians who were sure that their church was the "true church."

Most Christians have never had much of a problem in believing that the tomb was actually empty. The problem has always been, and still is, finding a way to "live it fully" as the early Christians did. In a world in which our way of life is threatened by radical religious violence, but also a world in which our acquisitiveness, materialism, and war-making are taken for granted, we're all running across slippery ice, trying to decide whether we should be like the hunter or the heretic. Which one are you trying to be? What kind of a church do we want, the violent church that killed Dirk Willems, or the non-violent church of Dirk Willems, along with that ancient company of those who lived the life of radical discipleship to which we are called by the empty tomb?

I've heard described in some funeral sermons would bore me to death—indeed, would seem like a kind of hell. Maybe you've also had to endure some of those funerals in which the preacher paints the obscene picture of a jolly get-together of old pals, where the weekly bridge game goes on, and our old crowd continues on forever. Such suggestions leave me asking, "Is this all there is?" What would seem spiritually responsible is that, if we have filled our lives with the noisy trash of this present world, we'll have to begin studying the good music of heaven. A real heaven might look like a music school in which we all learn to enjoy the symphonies of glory, the truly classical music and silence of heaven which will heal our wounds. As C. S. Lewis wrote, "Heaven is where all that is not music is silence."

But that image has always raised another question about such happy endings. Do the saints in glory spend all their time strumming their harps and singing their hallelujahs? Do they ever look down to see how we're doing? For that matter, are they even "up there?" Could it be that they surround our lives? The saintly John Chrysostom (349–407) wrote, "Open the eyes of faith and thou shalt behold a theatre of spectators, for if the air is filled with angels much more the church." He may have referred only to the angels, but the writer of the Letter to the Hebrews draws the picture of a great stadium in which the saints of all ages surround us like a "cloud of witnesses" (Heb 12:1), as though we are being cheered on in our race toward the finish line by a multitude of saintly spectators. I think that there's a good scriptural basis for believing that, in some way beyond our imagination, we are not alone in our journey, that there are friendly eyes and hopeful hearts watching us as we struggle onward. Sometimes we may even hear their songs of victory: "And when the fight is fierce, the warfare long, Steals on the ear the distant triumph song, And hearts are brave again, and arms are strong. Alleluia!"

What I hope for, above all, is to know more, "even as I have been fully known" (1 Cor 13:12). Robert Frost is reputed to have said that he had hope for the past, "that it will turn out to have been all right for what it was, something we can accept, mistakes made

Chapter 11

Home at Last

If this had been a formal treatise following the major points of the Apostle's Creed, we would arrive, finally, at those last words, "And the life everlasting." No statement about our faith would seem complete without sharing some thoughts about what we call heaven. From much that I've read, it appears that most of the world's religions have had to state, in some way, what they believe about "happy endings." I can't begin to talk about the subject without hearing my mother singing as she ironed our clothes,

> There's a land that is fairer than day,
> And by faith we can see it afar;
> For the Father waits over the way
> To prepare us a dwelling place there.
> In the sweet by and by,
> We shall meet on that beautiful shore;
> In the sweet by and by,
> We shall meet on that beautiful shore.

Even though my parents were no longer regular churchgoers, the hymns from childhood still sustained my mother. Some hope for happy endings has comforted persons of faith across the ages. The early Christians may not have sung such sentimental songs as ours, but they were sustained by the hope that, after their trials and tortures had ended, they would be at home with the Lord. Arriving "home at last," however we may sing about it, has been a favorite image of our final destination.

An interesting picture for this homecoming has been evolving in my mind. In the afternoon as I drive out to the charter school where I tutor Hispanic migrant farmworker children, I often end up following the school buses that transport other Hispanic children from public schools. If it happens to be a bus carrying elementary school students, the littlest ones make their exit from the bus as though they are being ejected. They run with joy, as though propelled from the bus, into the waiting arms of their mothers. However, if I happen to be following a school bus from a middle school, the exit of those older students is entirely different. They are not entirely happy about getting home. They are lugging backpacks heavy with homework; they don't run to their waiting parents with the reckless abandon of the little ones. I wonder which of these two homecomings offers the best imagery of the ending of our journey. Or could it be that there is some truth in both?

A dear friend and scholar envisions both possibilities. Those who have lived in the joy and freedom of God's radical grace and forgiveness will fly joyfully into the arms of our heavenly parent. Their long years in life's lower school will be over, and they will have graduated to the next higher academy. It is an encouraging picture, as I think of some of my aged friends beset with the infirmities of old age who, upon the moment of their death, will suddenly be like young high school graduates, eager and excited as they move on to the adventure of college or university. I hope that my mother's passing was like that. At age ninety-seven, blind, lame, and incontinent, but with her mind and memory crystal clear, she had outlived all her friends, and longed to "go home." She completed only the ninth grade before going to work at the collar shop as a young girl, but what a great surprise will await her as she moves on to a higher school!

It is, of course, difficult to believe that such a happy landing awaits everyone, especially those whose lives have been darkened by bad choices. However, because of God's unconditional grace,

they too will arrive "home at last." God's forgiveness is "for everyone, for everything, and for evermore," writes my scholarly friend. Yet, like those teenagers who get off the school bus with backpacks heavy with homework, those who have made bad choices—or have even lived evil lives—will experience this new life in the blinding light of God's heavenly presence as a difficult and demanding graduation. Homecoming, for them, will involve some kind of purgation or "catch up." They will start out behind the others who have lived a life of grace on earth. Could it be that those who have done their homework on earth will then have some kind of ministry in helping those who are behind as they make their way into the pure white light of eternity, becoming accustomed to their new life in heaven?

We can only make guesses at such questions. But what is sure is that we'll all be in school forever. Growth is the eternal order of our being as graciously adopted children of God. In that sense, our homecoming will be like that exhilarating time at the end of summer, when the keen and refreshing air of autumn signals our return to the campus and to the ongoing joys of learning. While some people picture heaven as a world of eternal spring, I wonder, instead, if heaven is the land of eternal autumn, that season of the year when we return to the halls of learning, as God's glory is "like a mantle spread o'er hill and dale in saffron flame and red." Whatever awaits us, one thing is sure: we'll all be in this exciting school of heavenly growth. What we pray for at our friends' passing will have come true; increasing in knowledge and love of God, we will go from strength to strength in the life of perfect service in God's heavenly kingdom.

It is difficult for me to think about a full quality of life without some of this good pain of growth. After all, some of the classes in this higher academy will be difficult and painful for each of us in different ways. I envision a curriculum in which I'll be given opportunity to make amends to those I've injured, learn what it was about me that made me thoughtless or offensive, and grow by grace into the true self I'm meant to be. That's the kind of purgation I need and want. Because of that, the kind of heaven that

by the selves we had to be, were not able to be, or perhaps what we wished, or what looking back half the time it seems we could so easily have been." It seems to me that heaven couldn't be really heaven unless, finally, I will be able to know who I really could have been, ought to have been, and who, eternally, I'm meant to be. Above all, I hope that, in the end, I'll be able to dismiss that bothersome "small me" who has always been tagging along beside me, the one whose embarrassing presence I seem unable to escape. Rabindranath Tagore wrote about that small self, "I came out alone on the way to my tryst. But who is this that follows me in the silent dark? I move aside to avoid his presence, but I escape him not. He makes the dust rise from the earth with his swagger; he adds his loud voice to every word I utter. He is my own little self, my lord, he knows no shame; but I am ashamed to come to thy door in his company." It will take nothing less than the grace of God to get rid of this false, troublesome part of my self. If it can happen in one fiery moment of grace, as some believe, that's fine. But if I must engage in some wrestling match as Jacob did at Bethel (Gen 32:24–30), I'm willing to take on that fight. I just want to be able to say a final farewell that annoying aspect of myself. Such a dispatch of that nasty, small self would make Heaven truly heavenly. At last, the little bird of my true self would be free.

One final picture helps me to think about what a happy ending might be, and it takes us back to the parable with which we began this long journey. As you remember, Jesus left my life's most important parable unfinished, with the elder son still outside the banquet hall. In my final imaginative scenario, he finally does relent and join the homecoming festivities. It is not until this point that both sons realize fully what they had not known before. What they realize now is that, long before the younger son had run off to the far country (just as the older son had lived far away from his father's heart in his proud perfectionism), they had always been living in the true heaven of their father's love. Heaven had always been surrounding them, even when they thought they had to find it elsewhere. Now they have really come home. In the end, love wins!

A Beautiful View

T. S. Eliot says it best for me:

> We shall not cease from exploration
> And the end of all our exploring
> Will be to arrive where we started
> And know the place for the first time.

Conclusion

A Life of Wordless Prayer

On June 23, 1954, I wrote to C. S. Lewis, asking him for his thoughts about the devotional life. Because of a passage in his novel, *Perelandra*, I wanted to know more of what he meant when he talked about daily prayers. I had read in a magazine article that Lewis answered all letters, no matter how inane, and so I thought that it was worth a try. Not too long thereafter, I received a hand-written letter from Magdalen College, Oxford, dated July 30, 1954.

> Dear Mr. Roberts, Thanks for your kind letter of the 23rd . . . . I am certainly unfit to advise anyone else on the devotional life. My own rules are (1) To make sure that, wherever else they may be placed, the main prayers should not be put "last thing at night." (2) To avoid introspection in prayers—I mean, not to watch ones own mind to see if it is in the right frame, but always to turn the attention outward toward God. (3) Never, never, to try to generate an emotion by will power. (4) To pray without words when I am able, but to fall back on words when tired or otherwise below par. With renewed thanks. Perhaps you will sometimes pray for me? Yours very sincerely, C. S. Lewis.

Many years later, fearing that this precious letter would somehow be lost upon my eventual demise, I donated it to Louisville Seminary, where it is mounted on a wall in the entrance to the seminary library. What I hope we can do, starting with this letter, is to somehow enter the inner life of this beloved author, and from there, think about the inner, contemplative life of another saintly soul whose life and writings have touched the world in some profound way.

My first reaction was to notice that Lewis prayed mostly "without words." How I wish I could have picked his brains on that practice. As he prayed, did he visualize the persons for whom he was offering intercessions? In other prayers of adoration and thanksgiving, like those in the Book of Common Prayer, did he read the words silently, or somehow hear them inwardly instead of whispering them? When I've tried copying his wordless way of prayer, it hasn't always worked. Sometimes I try to pray for people just by bringing their faces up on the screen of my mind. However, that doesn't always work because I find myself falling back into saying their name aloud or in a whisper. But maybe there's another way to think about this.

Over the years, these words of Lewis have taught me that our most important prayers are wordless. In fact, the basic language of prayer is always wordless. The prayers that get through to God are not so much those formed by our lips, but those that are uttered by our lives. How we live is how we pray!

To work on this idea let's move from Oxford, England in the twentieth century back to the first century in Caesarea Maritima, an important Roman outpost, a seaport thirty miles north of modern Tel Aviv. Stationed in this city is a Roman military officer named Cornelius, a centurion in command of 100 soldiers. Although he is technically a Roman pagan, Cornelius is living a very "un-Roman, un-pagan" way of life. When we read his story in Acts 10, we learn that Cornelius is a "god-fearer," a Gentile who is attracted and sympathetic to Judaism. He has not converted to Judaism, but what we notice is that he "gave alms generously to the people and prayed constantly to God" (Acts 10:2).

By the time we arrive at the end of Acts 10, in which his story is told, Cornelius will have become a baptized Christian—indeed, the first official Gentile convert to Christianity. But first we need to know that, as this chapter begins, Christianity is still a Jewish sect which has not been offered to Gentiles. At this point, all Christians are Jews. They do not believe that Jesus came to start a new religion for which they should build church buildings. They are still worshipping at the Temple because, in embracing Jesus, they believe that they are being faithful Jews. They do not call themselves Christians. For now, they are just simply Jews who believe in Jesus as their Messiah. Furthermore, they have no mission plan to share the good news with the Gentile world.

And what is particularly clear is that Peter, the chief apostle, has no plan for any such mission to the Gentiles. Indeed, what we learn is that nothing will happen until Cornelius reaches out to Peter. It's a long story that you can read for yourself, but notice how it begins with the prayers of Cornelius. Notice God's words to Cornelius: "Your prayers and your alms have ascended as a memorial before God" (Acts 10:4). Cornelius's prayerful and generous way of life is his prayer! The stewardship of our life's resources is constantly telling God what we really believe and what we really want. How we spend our time and money constitutes our real life of prayer, the wordless prayer of our life! How we live is how we pray! But now, back to C. S. Lewis.

We remember Lewis mostly as a prolific writer and scholar. Most of us know him for his delightful Narnia tales that we have shared with our children. But some of us who have made him our "hobby" know about his prodigious scholarship at Oxford and Cambridge. A few of us have read some of his more scholarly essays, but probably none of us have even opened his monumental works that were a part of the Oxford History of English Literature, such as *English Literature in the Sixteenth Century* or *Poetry and Prose in the Sixteenth Century*. Most readers of C. S. Lewis are probably unaware of these major works, not to mention many more scholarly works and papers.

However, those of us who have made his life our literary hobby know the other, mostly unnoticed story of his lifetime of care for an elderly woman. During all the years when the huge output of work was happening, he was taking care of an elderly woman in fulfillment of a promise he had made to her son who died in World War I. It all began at Keble College where Lewis and other cadets were being trained before being sent off to the Western Front. Because their names were alphabetically adjacent, his roommate was Edward Francis Courtenay Moore, known to his friends as Paddy. Before being sent off to different regiments, Lewis and Paddy made a solemn pact that, in the event of one or the other's death, the survivor would look after the parent of the one who had been killed. Even though they were only eighteen-year-old boys, this pact would shape the future life of C. S. Lewis. Paddy Moore was the one who died in the war, and Lewis became, thereafter, the caretaker of Paddy's mother, Janie Moore. It turned out to be a vow that would make most of his adult life one of domestic servitude.

There are different interpretations of this bizarre relationship, depending upon which biography of Lewis you choose to read. Did the relationship become romantic or intimate? We simply do not know—and we need to remember that, at this point, Lewis was an atheist, and not confined to any code of moral purity. What we know is that he kept the vow he had made. From the beginning, Lewis was involved in all the domestic tasks of cleaning, cooking, and shopping, in addition to helping Maureen, Paddy's younger sister, with her school work. As the years passed, however, Janie became an old woman, often bed-ridden, with persistent illnesses. Lewis would be called away from his desk to tend to tedious kitchen chores or, at night, see that Janie's bed was made before reading to her and saying good night. It was a life of domestic enslavement in which Lewis learned to accept interruptions as his "real life."

Against this daily routine of care for a demanding old woman, we can understand better what he meant when, many years later after he had become a Christian, he wrote to his lifelong friend, Arthur Greeves, "The great thing, if one can, is to stop regarding all the unpleasant things as interruptions of one's 'own' or 'real' life. The truth is of course that what one calls the interruptions are precisely one's real life—the life God is sending one day by day: what one calls one's 'real life' is a phantom of one's own imagination."

As Mrs. Moore's health and mental state worsened, she was finally moved to a nursing home in Oxford, the cost of which to Lewis was "crushing," until finally, on January 12, 1951, she died, with Lewis at her bedside. Notice: what had begun shortly after the First World War consumed the life of Lewis until after the end of the Second World War! Through all of this, Lewis had to contend with his brother Warren's deepening alcoholism. None of these burdens deterred Lewis's many acts of generosity to younger people in need of his help. He was unbelievably generous with his time and money. Nor did these burdens keep him from faithfully answering, by handwritten letters, such requests as that which he received from a young pastor in Newburgh, New York. His way of life reminds us again that how we spend our time and money is our real prayer, the wordless prayer of our life!

We each have different images of the life of C. S. Lewis. We may see him as the author of the books we've loved, or sitting with his friends, the Inklings, enjoying a pint at their favorite pub, or as a brilliant lecturer at Oxford or Cambridge. But the real story of his (and every) life is what he went home to every night. The quiet saintliness of Lewis, returning every night to the thankless task of caring for a demanding old woman is hardly ever noticed, although for Lewis it was the real life that God was sending to him day by day. What was the secret source of his strength? He shared his secret with us, and it becomes all the more revealing when we remember the burdens of his daily life. In *Beyond Personality*, he wrote:

> That's why the real problem of the Christian life comes where people don't usually look for it. It comes the very moment you wake up each morning. All your wishes and hopes for the day rush at you like wild animals. And the first job each morning is just shoving them all back; just listening to that other voice, taking that other point of

view, letting that other larger, stronger, quieter life come flowing in. And so on, all day. Standing back from all your natural fussings and frettings, coming in out of the wind.

This moment-by-moment, wordless discipline of silent surrender, of "coming in out of the wind," is the spiritual secret of the life of C. S. Lewis.

But let's look now at another saintly soul whose inner life was a wordless witness to the world. Probably more illiterate people on the face of the earth can now read because of the pioneer work of Frank C. Laubach (1884–1970). As a Congregational missionary, he chose to work among a remote and mostly illiterate Muslim tribe on the island of Mindanao in the Philippines. These Moros regarded the Christian Filipinos as their traditional enemies and, thus, seemed almost completely inaccessible to approach by a Christian missionary. But Laubach's approach to them was friendly, practical, and prayerful. In 1915, he developed a method of making literacy possible for illiterate people. It eventually became known as the "Each One Teach One" program and has been used to teach about 60 million people to read in their own language. Understandably, he became known as "The Apostle to the Illiterates." Just as important was that, during these years, he developed his own discipline of living, minute by minute, in the presence of God. He called it "The Game With Minutes."

But notice the basic, wordless spirituality of his approach. Frank Laubach came to believe that we can live constantly and prayerfully in the presence of God, and that the only way in which we can touch other lives in a positive and healing manner is by such constant, inner prayer. In his diary he wrote,

> I must confront these Moros with a divine love which will speak Christ to them though I never use his name. They must see God in me, and I must see God in them. Not to change the name of their religion, but to take their hand and say, "Come, let us look for God." . . . What right have I or any other person to come here and change the name of these people from Muslim to Christian, unless

I lead them to a life fuller of God than they have now?
Clearly, clearly, my job here is not to go to the town plaza
and make proselytes, it is to *live* wrapped in God, trembling to his thoughts, burning with his passion.

From this place of inner presence, his strategy for reaching
an unreachable people was to ask if he could study the Qur'an
with them. Did it work? Did he gain any converts? Probably not,
but who knows what the Spirit did? Who knows what seemingly
unreachable people pray in the secret, silent watches of the night?
We can never know what happens when those who are "deprived
of daylight, pray in the night." For that matter, what might such
prayerful friendliness accomplish if we, in this time of fear and
hostility, invited some Islamic teacher to come to our local church
to share with us some introduction to the Qur'an? If that sounds
like heresy to those readers who are evangelical Protestants, let
it be remembered that, after the invention of the printing press,
when the first printed edition of the Qur'an was published (1543),
the preface was written by Martin Luther!

I heard Laubach speak only once in 1955, and still have the
little booklet I picked up that night, *Letters By A Modern Mystic.* I
keep returning to it as a help in practicing a moment-by-moment
sense of the presence of Christ in my life. Many years later, a friend
and mentor of my teenage years, Dennis Kinlaw, became president
of Asbury College in Wilmore, Kentucky. He invited Laubach to
develop a department at the college devoted entirely to the practice
of prayer. In 1970, while I was in nearby Louisville, I invited Laubach to speak at my church. It was an invitation he had to refuse;
"as an old man," he still had a full speaking schedule. His letter was
written on April 27, 1970, and he would die forty-six days later on
June 11. He ended the letter with a final benediction for me, "God
give you a tremendous fire of the Spirit."

I have shared these final personal thoughts about these two
saintly souls as a conclusion to what we have been considering over
these pages about a friendlier faith because I believe that such a
faith will be communicated to our world only from a place of inner
prayer and contemplation. There are other saints whose lives could

have taught us the same lesson. I have limited my last thoughts to these two because of what their lives have taught me. Both lived with impossible circumstances: Lewis with an impossible home situation to which he returned every day for most of his adult life, Laubach to an impossible missionary assignment. But the secret of their lives was deep within "that other larger, stronger, quieter life." I don't think we can understand Lewis without realizing that it was that wordless, inner center of prayer that accounts for the depth of his spiritual genius. He even ended his letter to me with a prayer request, "Perhaps you will sometimes pray for me?"

What I have been hoping to say to you through these many pages is that you go out into a world that has been invaded by a friendly God, a world in which God's rule, God's kingdom of love and justice has "landed." There are other kings (and kingdoms) still purporting to run the world; their demise is just a matter of time. We are citizens of God's kingdom and its final victory is assured. Wherever we go in this present world, Christ is present. We live in a Christ-haunted, enchanted world. Every person you meet on every day is being pursued by the loving presence of Christ. That pursuit is going on in every life 24/7! God is doing the work; your task is to cooperate with what God is doing. Preaching is *not* your main task. When God needs your words, the opening will take place, and God will give you the few necessary words. What matters is that, in every contact on every day, with every person, you live "wrapped in God, trembling to his thoughts, burning with his passion." God will do the rest, in God's time, and in God's way.

Your daily life may seem very ordinary in contrast to what I am telling you. Indeed, the real world to which you return every night may be one in which you are a prisoner of some daily domestic drudgery or impossible situation, just as it was for Lewis. Or maybe some impossible soil may be resisting your best efforts to plant the seeds of the kingdom, just as it was with Laubach. But remember Jesus' words, "Be of good cheer, I have overcome the world" (John 16:33).

Long ago, I found some words that keep reminding me to maintain such a friendly, mirthful spirit. G. K. Chesterton wrote about Jesus, "I say it with reverence; there was in that shattering personality a thread that must be called shyness. There was something that He hid from all men when He went up a mountain to pray. There was something that He covered constantly by abrupt silence or impetuous isolation. There was some one thing that was too great for God to show us when He walked upon our earth; and I have sometimes fancied that it was His mirth." Go forth into the world in the mirth of the Christ who walks beside you, smiling!

Ideas for Group Study, Personal Reflection, and Additional Reading

Chapter 1—The Goal: A Friendlier Faith

Are you in general agreement with the goal of this book, that we need to make Christianity a friendlier faith? In your own experience, what aspects of Christian faith have you found unfriendly?

On the other hand, many of us have remained in the church because of some friendly experiences. What are some of the positive things that have kept you in the church? Who were some of the people along the way of your journey who made Christianity a friendly faith?

Although we have a long way to go through this book, what initial steps, in your opinion, need to be taken to make our faith friendlier?

In this chapter, there is a quotation from Eugene H. Peterson's introduction to the New Testament in his very helpful work, *The Message*. Readers may find it helpful to read some of the Scripture quotations in this book in Peterson's fresh rendering of biblical passages. *The Message* is available in several print formats and also in a Kindle format.

Chapter 2—Where It All Began

This is a necessary autobiographical chapter to let readers know about the author's spiritual journey. For readers who have been (or are) acquainted with life in a strict, fundamentalist church, some of it will be familiar. So, this chapter may assure them that the author has walked in their shoes. Other readers will find it interesting to learn how this book might never have been written had the author not had such early experiences.

In a group discussion of this chapter, it might be interesting for members to share some of the highlights of their own spiritual journey. In what ways has your journey been similar or different than that of the author?

One major turning point in the author's journey was his "accident" of finding a New Testament in his attic bedroom. Another turning point was in his high school biology class in which the assigned seating placed him next to another student with whom he would share his secret reading of the New Testament. Have there been any interesting "accidents" along the way, major turning points in your spiritual journey, occasions when you just happened to be in the right place at the right time? Who are some of the key people whose friendship has made all the difference in your relationship with God? As we remember and share such major influences upon our faith, we need to remember that, for some people, the faith journey has been a gradual experience since childhood. They can remember no big moments; for them, faith in Christ has been a way of life since childhood. They cannot imagine a life in which faith in Christ and worship in the church is not a regular, unquestioned way of life.

As we share our stories, let's remember that there is no one right and proper way to have come to faith in Christ. Sometimes it's a dramatic story, while at other times it's very ordinary. And the starting points can be very odd. For C. S. Lewis, the journey out of atheism to faith began on an early October day near sundown when he happened to pick up a book by George MacDonald in a railroad station bookstall. He was just looking for something to read on the train! He later wrote, "I had not the faintest what I had let myself in for by buying *Phatastes*." What beginning!

Chapter 3—We Know How the Story Ends

Homework: Scripture readings for this session are Luke 15:11–32 and Revelation 21:22–27.

In much of what we will be considering in every chapter, it's important to realize that much biblical truth is conveyed to us by metaphor, myth, or parable. Eternal truths can be made known to us only in symbols that show us what spiritual truth is like. For example, the question is not whether Jonah was actually swallowed by a whale many centuries ago, but rather what the story is trying to tell us about our life with God today. So, for starters, we need to realize that heaven and hell are not geographical places, but states of mind and heart that describe our relationship with God. This was even clarified for Roman Catholics (if they were listening) by Pope John Paul II in his news-making General Audience of July 28, 1999. Once heaven and hell become literal, physical places, they cease to convey their deep truth for our life today. We can live a heavenly, faithful life now, or else a hellish life apart from God.

What have been your thoughts about the traditional heaven/hell agenda that is proclaimed from many pulpits? How were your beliefs formed? Is your present faith the product of your family upbringing, or from teachers and preachers whose ministries helped shape your faith, or by your own reading and thinking? So, what are your thoughts or questions after reading this chapter?

How do you react to the unfinished ending of the parable in which, while the elder son refuses to join the banquet, the father remains with him in the outer darkness? What does this tell you about our heavenly Father?

In the passage from Revelation, what do you make of the promise that the gates of the holy city "will never be shut by day—and there will be no night there"?

Here's the bottom line: Do you want to live in the Holy City? The gates will never be shut (and are open right now) to those who live and pray every day, "Your kingdom come. Your will be done, on earth as in heaven." People who live that way are already in heaven. That's why Catherine of Sienna said, "It's heaven all the way to heaven." And, of course, it's hell all the way to hell. We're all on one or the other of these two roads, but can decide to change at any moment—like right now!

For those who want to dig deeper, a recommended reading is: *Inventing Hell: Dante, the Bible, and Eternal Torment*, by Jon M. Sweeney.

Chapter 4 -The Good News from the Garden of Eden.

Scripture homework for this chapter: Genesis 2:4b—3:24.

For those who have been taught the traditional interpretation of Genesis 3 as the story of the fall and the basis for the doctrine of original sin, this chapter may be something of a challenge. So, let's think about it by considering a question out of our own experience. Try thinking back upon the happiness you had with the birth of your children and how adorable they were as babies. But then reflect upon the fact that, as wonder-filled as their earliest years were for us, we certainly didn't want them to remain helpless infants forever. As enchanting as childhood innocence may be, we all agree that our little ones need to grow out of innocence into childhood, youth, and adulthood.

When you reflect upon this, you can see how Genesis 3 is *not* an account of something that actually happened in remote history, but instead a myth that tells us how things are and have always been. However human life may have developed over millions of years, we have always had to be people who learn and grow by making mistakes. Helpless infants have to grow out of their diapers and be toilet-trained. Babies must grow and move through their "terrible twos." Children must experience the pain and shame of self-awareness as they move into puberty, and all through this process they simply *must* make mistakes. Such experiences of painful growth are what Genesis 3 is about. We can't remain in a garden of innocence forever; we have to move out into the complicated life east of Eden. With this in mind, try remembering (or sharing with the group) the "growing pain" memories you recall during the growth of your children. Another helpful exercise will be to share memories of how you had to make some "good mistakes" in the course of your own growing up.

This exercise has taught us something important about the Bible: some of its stories are not history but, instead, mythical stories that contain deep truth about our life that is explained best by storytelling. However, we must avoid getting bogged down by treating these myths as history and then trying to find explanations of the historical problems in the stories. Because some ancient rabbis read Genesis 3 as history, they became entangled in the problem of why Adam did not die on the same day in which he ate the forbidden fruit, as God said he would (Gen 2:17). To solve this problem, they engaged in a wild chase for a scriptural solution. Finally, in Psalm 90:4 they found their answer: "For a thousand years in your sight are like yesterday when it is past, or like a watch in the night." There was their answer; Adam was living on an ancient time schedule when a day lasted 1,000 years. Thus, even though Adam lived for 930 years (Gen 5:5), according to the ancient 1,000-year day measurement, he actually did die late in the afternoon of the same day of his disobedience (*Jubilees* 4:29–30). You can see how we can miss the message of the Bible when we try to read every passage as literal history. With that in mind, what are the important, real-life lessons that you will take away from this chapter?

For those who want to dig deeper, an interesting Jewish viewpoint on Genesis 3 can be found in chapter 2 of *How Good Do We Have To Be?* by Harold S. Kushner. Another readable and scholarly discussion is in chapter 2 of *How To Read The Bible* by James L. Kugel.

Chapter 5—What Happened on the Cross?

Scripture homework: John 1:19–29, Luke 23:32–34, Psalm 50:7–23.

Before you had read this chapter, what did it mean to you when, partaking of Holy Communion, you heard the words, "This is the blood of Christ, shed for you," or other words describing Jesus as the "Lamb of God"?

In some churches, the death of Jesus is understood as a substitutionary action in which Jesus, the Son of God, had to die to save us from the wrath of God, the Father. As the chapter points out, this amounts to saying that Jesus died to save us from God! Doesn't this create an unbalanced view of the Trinity in which Jesus is more loving than our heavenly Father? How could such a father be thought of as "heavenly"? Then too, why would God be mad at us from the moment of our birth because, according to this theory, we are born infected with sin and incapable of pleasing God? It's like saying that we're lost from the moment of our birth, even though we didn't choose to be born. Can you make any sense of such an explanation of the cross?

To understand the cross as a demonstration of a love that will never give up on us liberates us to love the entire world as Jesus did in his forgiving death. If he "went down loving," so can we in our refusal to give up on any one of God's children. Instead of wondering whether others are "believers," we now know that God is a "believer" in every person, and is pursuing every human life. God's love is inescapable; sooner or later, we will be caught by the love that never gives up. How might all of this change your celebration of Holy Communion and make it relevant to your relationship with your neighbors?

For those who want to read more about this question, a helpful book was written in 1945 by the eloquent British preacher, Leslie Weatherhead, entitled, *A Plain Man Looks At The Cross: An Attempt to Explain, in Simple Language for the Modern Man, the Significance of the Death of Christ.*

Chapter 6—The Great Dinner Dance: The Trinity

Scripture homework for this chapter: Genesis 1:1–2:4a, Genesis 18:1–15.

Many years ago, my sermons could be heard weekly by a radio audience in most of the eastern United States via radio station KDKA, Pittsburgh. It was a very diverse audience from which I received both friendly and unfriendly mail. I was often surprised by the breadth of my radio congregation, like the time when I learned that, on every Sunday evening, a group of Roman Catholic nuns ended their day by listening to my sermons. It was humbling to know that I had such regular radio friends. But it wasn't always that way.

A letter arrived shortly after I had delivered a sermon about the incident in Luke 2:41–52, when Jesus was accidently separated from his parents and was lost for three days. I gave that sermon the title, "The Lost Boy," which was the title that the revered Henry Van Dyke gave to his short story about the same incident. The writer of the letter was not only offended by the sermon title, but had talked with Jesus about it. According to the Jesus with whom she talked each day, she informed me that Jesus had told her that he had never been lost. And so, with the authority of Jesus' own words to her, she finished her letter by telling me, "You, Morgan Roberts, are the lost boy!"

I'm guessing that there were other listeners out there in radioland who might have had the same reaction to my sermon. There were not only friendly nuns in my audience; there were probably many Protestants who had their own daily "little talks with Jesus" who hadn't bothered to write to me. Interesting, isn't it, how many Christians talk mostly with Jesus, sometimes with their heavenly Father, but seldom with the Holy Spirit! For them, Jesus has mostly taken over the job is listening to our prayers. In a truly Trinitarian understanding of God, as one of my choir directors once said, "All three of them are listening."

My real concern with the lady's angry letter, however, is not with her "little talks with Jesus," but with her assumption that Jesus was on her side and not on mine. It is, of course, an assumption that can be made by any of us, even the most scholarly, when we are absolutely sure that we are in sole possession of the true faith. E. B. White once characterized the chummy religion offered by some preachers as, "You Can Be Jehovah's Pal." The problem of being a special pal of Jesus is that we can so easily assume that "we" are the insiders and "they" are the outsiders—or the "lost boys."

I had a Trinitarian purpose when I let my wild imagination create another possible closing scene for the parable in the Prodigal Son. When the father, mother, younger son, and reluctant older brother return to the big party and find that it has been crashed by the questionable friends that the younger son had made in the far country, I was trying to say that the far country was not outside of the father's love. Ordinarily, when we preach about that parable, we stress the fact that the younger son, even in the far country, was never outside of his father's loving heart. That's certainly a good rendering of Luke's message; however, when we add John's understanding of God as always Trinitarian, always the presence of God as Father, Son, and Holy Spirit, we realize that, with God, there is no far country. There is no faraway place in which God does not have "other sheep." So, when I have my "little talks with Jesus" (or however else I may offer my prayers), I must remember that God is always hearing the prayers, spoken or unspoken, of all the children of God. There is no "us vs. them" in God's Trinitarian presence.

No one has been orphaned, abandoned, by our God. God has no orphans, only beloved children. So, while I may find comfort in the ways suggested in this chapter, as a Friend who is always with me, or as an uninvited Guest at every table, I must not forget that God is the transcendent Father above of every life, the Christ who walks alongside on every pathway, and the indwelling Spirit in every heart. The best homework you can do in considering this chapter is to start thinking differently about someone else in your neighborhood. Pick just one person and, when you talk with them in the coming week, remember that God is looking down upon them with Fatherly love, that Jesus, the Christ is standing beside them, and that the same Spirit who mysteriously indwells your heart is also living in their heart. Just try it, and keep a record of how this changes your relationship with them.

For those who want to dig deeper, read: *The Divine Dance: The Trinity and Your Transformation*, by Richard Rohr with Mike Morrell. For a fictional approach to the Trinity, if you haven't seen the movie, then try reading *The Shack*, by William Paul Young, about which, Eugene Peterson, author of *The Message*, has said, "The book has the potential to do for our generation what John Bunyan's *Pilgrim's Progress* did for his. It's that good!"

Chapter 7—I Like You Just the Way You Are

Scripture homework: Philippians 2:1–12.

When I lived in Pittsburgh, I lived in *Mister Rogers Neighborhood*, but in a way far more real than those who experience that neighborhood only on TV. I lived in Fred Rogers's real neighborhood. His TV studio was down the street, only a few blocks away, and his condominium was a short walk up the hill. Fred often walked by my house and, on one day, stopped by unannounced for a visit. It just happened that my young grandchildren were visiting on that day so that, when the doorbell rang, Christopher, aged 5, ran to the door and opened it. There, to his astonishment, was the real Mister Rogers. He was so speechless that, despite Fred's friendliness, he could not respond to his questions. When Fred had finished his visit with me, I asked Christopher what he thought about Fred's visit. His response was, "I thought he lived in another country." For Christopher, Mister Rogers lived in the other country of the TV screen, not in the country of a regular neighborhood. And that's the way most of us think about Jesus, despite the scriptural assertion of John 1:14, that "he moved right into the neighborhood." So, here's a question to ponder: How differently would you feel if Jesus lived right in your neighborhood, on your street, in your apartment/condominium complex, or in your retirement community? How would this change your feelings about yourself? What would you want to do differently? Would you feel better or worse about yourself? And above all, how would your life be different if you realized that, no matter what, Jesus liked living near you every day? How does this make you feel about your neighbors? As you do this, reflect upon the Scripture homework for this lesson that reminds us that God is "at work in you, enabling us to will and to work for his good pleasure." Keep some daily notes as you think about these questions and thoughts and, if appropriate, share them with the group with whom you are studying this book.

If God, as the Scripture suggests, is at work on your life so that you are "a work in progress," what have been some of the experiences in which you have experienced his chiseling and carving? Have some of your difficult neighbors been a part of this painful, but necessary, process?

Thinking about the experience of Thomas Merton, and the words of Charles F. Andrews, could you ever consider your own neighborhood something like the family of God, even though many of your neighbors may not be churchgoing people? What prevents you from believing that "the gate of Heaven is everywhere"?

Those who want to read Merton's entire statement about his experience of perceiving the presence of God in every human life can find it in his *Conjectures of a Guilty Bystander*, pages 156 to 158.

Chapter 8—Jesus, the Extraordinary Ordinary

We've come a long way from Jesus and his poor, ordinary family. They were so poor that they had lost their property, so that Joseph was reduced to working for other people as a *tekton*, something like a construction worker. After the birth of Jesus, because of their poverty, they brought a minimal offering of turtledoves or pigeons (Luke 2:24) to the Temple (as allowed by Lev 12:8). How did we ever get to the point where we built huge, expensive cathedrals in which priests minister in elaborate liturgical vestments, all in the name of the penniless Jesus? It is hard to imagine Jesus, Mary, and Joseph coming back to visit some of today's beautiful and opulent places of worship. In many of them, where we worship in our

Sunday finery, the holy family would not be greeted with enthusiasm. Mistaking them for the poor who come to our churches for free food, instead of seating them in the sanctuary, we might direct them to the location of our food pantry.

Of course, not all Christians have followed this tradition of luxurious discipleship. Such monastic figures as Benedict and Francis rebelled against the grandiose proportions of the church in their day. Many years later, such groups as the Quakers, Mennonites, and Amish opted for a simpler way of life. They still dress simply, and their places of worship are plain. All of them were able to see that a superhuman image of Jesus was *not* where the New Testament was taking us. But where do we go with all of this? It's too late for some of us to dismantle our fancy sanctuaries; that would be wasteful. And an austere, plain and simple wardrobe wouldn't work for those of us who must follow certain dress codes in our place of business. So how do we return to the ordinary simplicity of the Jesus whom we profess to follow?

We will each have different responses to this challenge. Many of us will attempt to simplify our way of life, reordering our priorities, so that we can direct more of our money to the needs of the poor. We will, in the words of Dorothy Day, seek to "live simply so that others can simply live." Others, in addition to the stewardship of our money, will find some way to invest our time so that we have a more "hands-on" contact with those, who in our day, are living in the same poverty in which Jesus and his family lived. Whatever our response may be, we must always remember the extraordinary ordinary way of Jesus.

What we must consider today is that Jesus lived his extraordinary life with the same human equipment that is ours. He was truly one of us in every way. What else could it mean when we read that "the Word was made flesh," and that Jesus "in every respect has been tempted as we are" (Heb 4:15)? Jesus was not "out of touch with our reality" (*The Message*). Whatever may be our level of education or our financial position, we have all that we need to follow him. Jesus is "followable." By God's grace, we *can* do it. "Just as I am" I can say "yes" to God's will for me today.

Chapter 9—What About Evangelism and Being Born Again?

Scripture homework: John 3:1–10. It will be helpful to read this in the New Revised Standard Version, giving attention to the literal rendering, "born from above" in verse 3, and also to the footnote concerning the plural pronoun, "you" in verse 7.

This chapter will require some mind-stretching for those who have been taught that being born again is the heart of the Christian message, and that it's all based upon John 3:16. So it will be important to read the passage with references to the notes above.

Another new learning that will challenge our previous understandings of this fourth Gospel is the fact that it reflects a situation when the followers of Jesus were all Jews. They did not yet have their own places of worship or church buildings. They were not yet called Christians, and they were still worshipping in synagogues alongside other Jews. However, as the chapter notes, some of them were being excluded from the synagogues and told that they could not be faithful Jews because of their new faith in Jesus. It may be difficult for us to wrap our minds around such a situation, but we really can't get into the heart of the Gospel of John until we do. Because of this, the statement in John 14 about Jesus being "the way" is not applicable to our relationship with other faiths today. It is speaking to the particular situation of these first-century Jewish believers, called Nazarenes.

This chapter demands some rethinking about missionary efforts, particularly in the nineteenth century, to evangelize persons of other religions in other nations. The chapter offers some other ways of thinking about some of the unrecognized successes of such world evangelism. We need to wrestle with questions of how this might change our view about persons of other faiths in our own neighborhood. We nearly all have Jewish neighbors, and nowadays we may also have Muslim or Hindu neighbors. Pew Research indicates that the present Muslim population of 3.3 million people will expand by 2050 to 8.1 million to exceed the Jewish population.

By that same year, the projection is that the Hindu population will almost equal the Jewish population. So, what does all say about our relationship as Christians to the growing religious diversity of our own neighborhood?

For those who want to dig deeper into these issues, two books might be helpful. *The Community of the Beloved Disciple,* written by a distinguished American New Testament scholar, Raymond E. Brown, is an excellent small work for understanding the Gospel of John. Another readable work for understanding our own faith in relationship with other faiths is *The Wide, Wide Circle of Divine Love: A Biblical Case for Religious Diversity.* It comes to us from a world-class Old Testament scholar, W. Eugene March.

Chapter 10—The Evidence for the Empty Tomb

Scripture homework: Acts 4:32–37, Matthew 5:44,45, Luke 6:35,36.

This could be the most difficult chapter in the entire book. It could "spoil" our future celebrations of Easter because, instead of asking whether we believe in the empty tomb, it addresses our way of life, asking whether we would dare to live as though the resurrection really did happen.

Before we get into the difficulties of "living" the resurrection as the early Christians did, let's share how we have previously thought about it. What do you think happened on the first Easter morning? How do you explain the fact that the accounts differ? For example, Paul's statement about the resurrection in 1 Corinthians 15 is the earliest account, written decades before the first Gospel, Mark. According to Paul, the risen Christ appeared to Peter and the twelve (verse 5); however, according to John's gospel, Mary Magdalene was the first witness to the resurrection. Then, according to Mark, the Risen Jesus didn't even make an appearance, but a "young man, dressed in a white robe" told the women to go and tell his disciples and Peter that Jesus would see them in Galilee, after which the women left the tomb in fear. How would you explain these discrepancies to someone who interprets documents literally?

But now here's the big problem. The significance of the resurrection was so shattering to the earliest Christians that they renounced their property and lived in a communal manner. Unless we make a radical decision to leave our present church and join some communal order, we're probably not going to follow their example. It's just impossible. But some Christians, recognizing the impossibility of returning to such communal living, have adopted radical simplicity as their way of life. It's not all that complicated to live by some of their rules. Here are some of them. Do I have to buy the latest model of every article I presently own? If my present car is running safely, and if I do not need to travel long distances to earn a living, why can't I drive an old car? Why do I have to own the latest version of my mobile phone? Why do I need a closet with more clothing than I need, unless a certain weekly change of attire is required for my work? Why do I have to eat out at restaurants when I can eat more healthily and less expensively at home? When something I own wears out, why can't I replace it with a used item? The list is endless, but when you apply such questions to most of the "stuff" we own or the activities in which we engage, it becomes difficult to justify much of our present lifestyle in a world in which so many people are hungry.

The most vibrantly happy couple I've ever known made a radical decision early in their married life. Because they had not been blessed with children, they decided to tithe in reverse: to live on 10 percent of their income and give 90 percent away to the Lord's work. One of their accomplishments was that, because they had no children of their own, they created and funded a summer camp for children, especially needy children—and that was just one of the things that their simple lifestyle made possible. Who knows how much you could accomplish if you attempted to simplify your life in an even minimal manner as a copy of the early Christian response to the resurrection!

Becoming "Easter People" becomes even more difficult when you consider the non-violent lifestyle of the early Christians who

literally followed the command of Jesus to love their enen
even prayed for those who "fed them to the lions." If the
impossible, it's worth remembering that such forgiving lc.
brought the Roman Empire to its knees. It brings to mind what
Fred Rogers was taught by his favorite seminary professor, William Orr, who told him that there was one word that evil could
never withstand—and that word was "forgiveness."

Chapter 11—Home at Last

The "dear friend and scholar" to whose work I refer in this chapter
is Dr. J. Harold Ellens. For those who want to learn more about the
radical implications of unconditional grace, I recommend reading
his book, *By Grace Alone: Forgiveness for Everyone, for Everything,
for Evermore.*

One of the most helpful ways to think about heaven is to remember your friends and loved ones who are already there. Some
Christians have "saints' days" upon which they remember the heroic followers of Jesus who have been officially canonized. Even
if your church doesn't have such a practice, it can be helpful to
make a list of those who have been special saints in your life. Your
selection of such saints will be turn out to be interesting. Some
will have been highly educated and well-known, while others may
have lived lives of near-poverty and simplicity. It can be helpful to
have one day every week when you remember them. Another way
to remember them is to take one of them with you throughout an
entire day. If you can think of them as walking with you throughout an entire day, you'll find it interesting how differently you
may react to interruptions and other frustrations. When you're
tempted to be angry, their peaceful, patient presence will restrain
you. Whether you remember them weekly, or take one of them
with you on certain days, there's a Jewish prayer you might want
to offer as you remember them. "May God remember forever my
dear ones who have gone to their eternal rest. I see them now with
the eye of memory, their faults forgiven, their virtues grown larger.
So does goodness live, and weakness fade from sight. I remember

them with gratitude and bless their names. May they be at one with the One who is life eternal. May the beauty of their lives shine for evermore, and may my life always bring honor to their memory."

As we come to realize more fully our common identity will all persons as children of God and, thus, our identity with the multitude of faithful souls who surround us in the eternal world, our experience may be like that of Thomas Merton, who realized the gate of heaven is everywhere. If we live with this present heavenly realization, when we pass from this world into God's eternal presence, we'll know that, all along, we were in heaven. Spend some time reflecting upon our opening parable with this thought in mind. Both sons were always in the heaven of their father's love. Maybe when we finally get home, we'll realize that we were always there. We'll realize that we were always living in a place with a beautiful view. We'll see, as did Jacob, that we were always living in an "awesome place," close to "the gate of heaven" (Gen 28:17). Or, as T. S. Eliot wrote, we will "arrive where we started and know the place for the first time."

Conclusion—A Life of Wordless Prayer

In the first draft of this little book, this was not the closing chapter. The subject of prayer was dealt with in another way in an earlier chapter. As the book evolved and changed, however, what became clear is that, all along, to develop a friendlier Christianity, we were moving toward a life of contemplative prayer. When I asked the question, "How then shall we live?" I kept coming back to a life in which action is based upon and surrounded by a prayerful life.

So, the only homework for this chapter is that you begin writing your own answer to the question, "How then shall I live?" In doing so, try to reflect upon the chapters of this book that have been the most challenging, or the most enlightening, or the most comforting for you. What concrete decisions will you make about your future? Or else, what new ways of living will you try? Remember that you can always revise your plan or change your mind—and also that you'll make mistakes. The important thing is to keep trying. So, remember the epitaph of a Swiss mountaineer who was never seen again as he tried to make it to the top of a great mountain, "When last seen, he was climbing upward!"

Made in the USA
Lexington, KY
20 March 2019